A few summers ago my wife Donna Lee and I were returning from vacationing in the panhandle of Idaho. As we drove across a long, flat, hot stretch of road in Eastern Washington, a thought occurred to me. I asked Donna Lee to hand me my portfolio from the back seat. I drove with one knee as I scribbled down this paragraph:

"There lives inside each of us a genius, a power, a capacity—an untapped potential. This possibility for being and becoming is seen in the shadows of our past achievements—the mist of our dreams and aspirations. We tap our potential by gaining confidence from our achievements, accepting responsibility for our present and committing to our goals."

I haven't changed a word of that scribbled paragraph since I first wrote it down. *How to Turbo-Charge You* is based on this philosophical statement. The goal of this book is to show you how you can identify *your potential*, get in touch with *your strengths*, clarify *your dreams* and commit to *your goals*.

How To Turbo-Charge You
Six Steps to Tap Your True Potential

You are about to read a book that will help you maximize every success, leverage every failure, and manage your momentum for maximum mileage.

We are not merely the product of our experiences. We are the product of our experiences as filtered through the reflective lens of our eyes. If we were just the product of our experiences, every person who experienced the same circumstances would come out of those circumstances acting, looking and being the same way. And yet we have all seen examples of people who have come from education and wealth who are narrow, stingy, selfish, plagued with fear and worry, barely able to live from day to day, and, as a result, have ended up derelicts. We have seen examples of people who have come from poverty and squalor who have developed into beautiful, graceful, caring, generous people who are highly successful and enjoy real prosperity.

Mind is the master power that molds and makes.
And man is mind, and evermore he takes
The tools of thought and shaping what he wills
Brings forth a thousand joys, a thousand ills.
He thinks in secret and it comes to pass.
Environment is but his looking glass.

James Allen, *As a Man Thinketh*

How To
Turbo-Charge You

Six Steps
to Tap Your True Potential

Larry W. Dennis

Rising Tide Publishing
Portland, Oregon

How To Turbo-Charge You
Six Steps to Tap Your True Potential

Rising Tide Publishing
5440 SW Westgate Drive, Suite 340
Portland, Oregon 97221

ISBN 0-9631766-2-5
Library of Congress No. 94-66365

Acknowledgement
The quotation on pages 189-190 is from *It Was On Fire When I Lay Down On It* by Robert Fulghum, copyright © 1988, 1989 by Robert Fulghum. Reprinted by permission of Villard Books, a division of Random House, Inc.

Manufactured in the U.S.A.

This book is dedicated to the memory of my good friend Jack Boland who, more than any other person, helped me fully understand and apply the "Turbo-charging" principles to myself and my family, enabling us to successfully tap more of our potential.

Foreword

by Monte Shelton

I first began driving small race cars in 1960. I'd become very accustomed to the torque/thrust responsiveness of a normal aspirated engine. Then, in 1976, I drove my first turbo-charged G. T. race car. In spite of the fact that I intellectually knew about the added responsiveness, I was astounded and found that I had a decided competitive advantage which exceeded my expectations.

The most astounding thing for me about the turbo-charger was the limited additional investment that was required to achieve this new level of performance. With relatively few modifications to the engine, performance was improved over 50%.

Larry Dennis has captured in his new book, *How to Turbo-Charge You,* a system and strategy that you can employ to improve your own performance by 50%. As a result, you can experience the same competitive advantage that I experienced as a race car driver. How do I know? Why do I say this? Because I have learned and utilized the same principles Larry presents in his book over the years in my own life. I discovered these principles through trial and error; you can take advantage of the turbo-charger principle more easily. They are outlined in a systematic way, and they're easy to follow, so you can take the steps necessary to leverage off your past performance and to clarify your objectives. The good news is you don't have to add dramatically to your stature, intellect or basic knowledge. In other words, you don't have to go back to college.

So, as we say in racing, suit up, put on your helmet, put on your safety harness and be ready for the ride of your life! Obviously there are far more people who have said, "I'd love to drive a race car," than there are those who ever do. *How to Turbo-Charge You* will take your fleeting wish or desire to crystallization of the goal, and put together an action plan to make your dreams come true. Reading this book alone will turbo-charge your performance. Larry leaves little to interpretation or your imagination. All you have to do is simply follow the steps to tap your potential and you'll experience the winning feeling that race car champions know as youl win first place in your own race to achieve your heart's desire.

Monte Shelton, winner of five Trans-Ams,
Chairman of the Board, Monte Shelton Motor Co.

Table of Contents

Part One

Six Steps
to Tap Your True Potential

Introduction

When we compare ourselves to what we could be, it is like comparing the ocean waves to its mighty, untapped depths.
         — Ralph Waldo Emerson

The Promise

This year can be the greatest year of your life. You can be a more effective leader, a superior salesperson, a better parent. You can make more money and experience greater fulfillment and joy in every area of your life. You can experience a new sense of direction, the feeling of being in the driver's seat of your life for the rest of your life. What's more, it's easy. This book will show you how to apply a simple six-step process that will make this year the most exciting year of your life and will direct the rest of your life steadily upward. I call the process "Turbo-charging," because it takes advantage of all the skills, talents, intuition and energy you already have but have not fully used.

The Metaphor

In the early 1930s superchargers were first used on high-performance cars like Auburns and Cords. High-performance, direct-driven superchargers are still popular today on all the fastest drag boats and cars. The use of exhaust-driven turbo-chargers in the 1980s grew out of the necessity to find more economic ways to power high-performance engines during and after the oil embargo. The success of turbo-charging engines resulted in up to 30% of all new cars sold being turbo-charged. The term is synonymous with efficiency, high-performance, and making the most of existing resources.

Turbo-chargers provide us with up to 50% more power by taking advantage of the engine's exhaust. Previously, exhaust was thought of as a pollutant, something worse than useless. To put it to use, some of the exhaust is re-routed. The re-routed exhaust spins a turbine, driving a vacuum pump that draws fresh, pre-compressed air into the combustion chamber of the engine's cylinder. As a result, the compression ratio is dramatically improved. By utilizing the exhaust's untapped potential, and without adding any additional size or capacity to the engine, performance and output is increased by as much as 50%. *What had been wasted, what had always been there, now significantly boosts the engine's power.*

The Analogy

Can you turbo-charge yourself? Can you significantly improve your performance and the quality of your life using what had previously been wasted? What if you're already doing a great job and are pleased with what you've accomplished? What about your age, physical limitations, inherited characteristics, and intelligence quotient? Is it really possible to increase your performance by 50% and experience a more abundant life?

Or, are you so limited by your age, education, physical stature, family heritage, background and experience that you are prevented from achieving your dreams, ambitions, hopes and desires?

Well...consider these examples:

- Napoleon Bonaparte was only 5'6" tall...

- The average Olympic competitor is 5'9"...

- Oprah Winfrey overcame an emotionally traumatic childhood to become one of the most successful media personalities ever...

- Bill Gates dropped out of Harvard to start Microsoft...

- Helen Keller, blind, deaf and mute at two years of age learned to read, write, and speak. She devoted her life to helping the blind and deaf...

- Many character actors you see in popular television shows didn't get their "start" until middle age or later...

- John Milton wrote *Paradise Lost* in spite of being blind and sick...

- Ben Hogan returned to golf four years after a terrible car wreck and a prognosis that he would never walk again—he later won three top golf tournaments...

- Tom Dempsey became a place kicker in professional football despite being born without a right hand and with only part of his right foot...
- Ludwig Von Beethoven composed his best music following his total deafness...
- F. D. Roosevelt, a polio victim, served four terms as President...
- And, certainly, Stephen Hawking's incapacities resulting from cerebral palsy did not stop his great thinking, including his breakthrough work, *A Brief History of Time*...

Let's be honest. Certainly, some lack of education, physical attributes, age, family heritage or emotional concerns can potentially limit us, hold us back and result in us being also-rans. The question remains: Do *you* have more potential than you are using, tapping, capitalizing on? And, do you care?

Overcoming Obstacles to High Performance

In 1982 I bought my 1978 Porsche-911SC. It only had 15,000 miles on it, and looked as if it had never been driven. I couldn't find a scratch on it. While I'd been driving a Jaguar-V12XJS for a number of years before this, I was immediately amazed at the high performance and torque of the Porsche's 6-cylinder engine.

I loved driving the car from the very first day. One day, after I'd been driving the car for about two years I took it to the shop for an oil change and regular maintenance. When I came back to pick it up, my mechanic said, "Larry, while we were working on your car, we discovered a bolt that someone must have put on the accelerator. Like a governor, it eliminates the possibility of fully accelerating. We took it off. I hope you don't mind."

I said, "Of course, not." When I drove the car home that day I could not believe the additional power, punch, and get-up-and-go I got from my Porsche! I had enjoyed driving the car previously, but now it was like having a brand new vehicle. The lesson I learned from this experience is that even though I may think my life is full, there is a lot more potential available to me if I can remove the "governors" of fear, inhibition, and self-effacement.

- At the turn of the century, William James, the father of American psychology, said, *"The average person only uses 10% of his ability."* What would you be like if you could tap into that unused 90% of *your* ability?

• Einstein estimated that *he* only used 10% of his potential.

• UCLA's BRI (Brain Research Institute), after extensive research, concluded that we use less than 1% of our eighteen trillion brain cells.

Tapping Your Potential

The real question is, *"Do you want to use more of your potential?* Oh, I know you've been distracted; I know you've had problems. We *all* have problems. But just as the "oil embargo" resulted in the practical use of the turbo-charger, your problems can lead you to new self-discoveries. If you approach your problems with a positive mental attitude they can become a blessing in disguise! Think of the many problems and setbacks you have already overcome. The greatest asset anyone can possess is *a desire for knowledge* and *the willingness to earn it.* Every adversity carries with it the seed of an equivalent benefit. So, let's not look for excuses. If you're ready to find ways of reaching your untapped potential, *read on.*

Chapter 1

How to Tap Your Potential

"There lives inside each of us a genius, a power, a capacity—an untapped potential..."

I know one thing about you already: you are not satisfied. If this were not true, you would not be reading this book. In the larger sense, all vital human beings are dissatisfied with the status quo. We know somehow that there must be more. You don't have to be sick to get better. Unfortunately, some people seem to think so and the only time they reach out to grab more of their true potential is in times of crisis. This is a reactive approach to life, personal growth and development. *How to Turbo-Charge You* will show you how to be proactive in making the most out of what God gave you. When can our good be the enemy of our better? Anytime we become *self-satisfied* and *complacent.*

The Chinese character for "crisis" consists of the elements meaning "danger" and "opportunity." Life is made of the same combination of ingredients. Whether danger or opportunity predominates depends on how you approach challenges.

What's Stopping You?

Have you ever gone to the circus or the zoo and noticed an elephant tethered by a 3" thick rope to a 24" stake? That elephant could pull the stake out of the ground, snap that rope in half, go anywhere it wanted to. Then why doesn't it try? When it was a calf, the elephant was tethered by the same rope, and held down by the same stake. It struggled and struggled with all of its might, until it finally learned that the struggle was useless. It could not pull the stake out. It could not break the rope. Having learned its lesson well, the elephant conceded to being restrained by the seemingly unlimited force of the tether.

True enough, when the elephant was a calf it couldn't pull up the stake, but now that it is fully grown, it could easily walk away. The elephant, however, is stuck in its belief system. In its mind, the elephant thinks it cannot break free, and therefore it does not even try.

How are you limiting yourself? There may have been a time when, physically, you couldn't do certain things. Perhaps you couldn't achieve certain goals because of your limited education or experience. Perhaps these limitations were planted in your mind by well-intentioned friends, relatives, parents, or siblings. Now it is time to challenge your belief system, and not limit yourself by what you may have been programmed to think is true for you.

Shifting Gears

A number of years ago Donna Lee and I went to Barbados, in the West Indies, to conduct sales and leadership skills training classes. It was a wonderful assignment and we were thoroughly enjoying ourselves on the small Caribbean Island when it occurred to me that we would have even more fun if we had our own transportation instead of relying on friends or public transportation. I decided to rent a small Suzuki motorcycle.

I arrived at the motorcycle livery at noon. The regular staff was out to lunch, but I've driven motorcycles since I was fifteen and was sure I could handle the bike without special instructions even though I had never driven a Suzuki. I asked the fellow at the livery, "Is low gear all the way down or all the way up?"

He said, "It's all the way up."

In order to get my Baijen driver's license I had to drive the motorcycle through a series of obstacles. As I was going through the obstacles—a series of garbage cans they had set up for me to maneuver between—I thought to myself, "This is going to be great! It's small, maybe 80cc's, but I can put Donna Lee on the back and we can run all around the island. We're going to have a great time!"

After going through the obstacles satisfactorily, I went into the police station, paid my three dollars, got my driver's license, got on the motorcycle, pulled out of the parking lot and into the traffic flow, and, for the first time, I shifted. If you're familiar with a Suzuki you know what happened next. I discovered I had been in fourth gear all the time. By shifting down into low gear I could literally do a wheely on that little motorbike! Even though I could ride the bike well enough in fourth gear, when I discovered how much more zip I could muster in second and third gear, I got really excited!

The average person travels through life experiencing some degree of satisfaction using only half the get-up-and-go, the lift-power, available to them. When you discover how to "shift gears," you'll tap into your true potential. And when you discover that potential you'll live your life with a zest that will exceed anything you've enjoyed before.

Personalize Your Potential

I've conducted Leadership programs for the past twenty-five years, and at the first session I ask class members to think of someone—a spouse, sibling, boss or subordinate—who is living below their potential; someone who clearly sells themself short. No one has ever responded with a blank look on their face; no one has ever said, "I can't think of anyone." I usually ask my students to tell me their relationship to the person they've thought of, just to be sure they have someone clearly in mind. I'd like you to take this exercise with me right now. Who comes to your mind when you think of un-realized potential? (Please do not read further until you have thought of a person clearly living below his or her potential. Write that person's initials in the space provided below. Use pencil, in case you decide to loan that person this book.)

_____

If you could tell that person something, what would you say to help them get a greater glimpse of their potential?

_____

_____

Now, if that person, or someone else in your acquaintance, were reading this book would they have thought of you if they were asked the same question?

The reason for this exercise is to get past your intellectually detached and depersonalized textbook agreement that, yes, "people" do indeed have greater potential than "they" realize. Arrive at the point where you can say, "Yes, *I* have more potential than *I* am using."

I am not asking you to think of yourself negatively. There's no reason to sell yourself short. Up your belief in the most important person in the world by acknowledging, "No matter how well I am doing, how successful I am, I can do better."

Died, age 20; buried, age 60

This is the sad epitaph of many. Mummification sets in at an age when they should be ripping the world wide open. By way of contrast, consider this man, the founder of a world famous university:

- At the age of twenty-five, he founded the first subscription library in America.

- Now, think fire. While still a young man, he started the first fire department, invented the lightning rod, designed a heating stove that is still in use today.

- By the time he was forty-one, he was an established author, printer and publisher.

- He invented bifocals when he was seventy-eight.

These accomplishments scarcely begin to describe this famous wit, conversationalist, economist, philosopher, and diplomat. A favorite in the capitals of Europe, Benjamin Franklin was a linguist who spoke and wrote five languages. He was an advocate of paratroopers (from balloons) a century before the airplane was invented. An ambassador, statesman, and gazetteer, he remained active and vital until he died at age eighty-four.

And yet, Benjamin Franklin had exactly two years of formal schooling. It's a good bet you already have more sheer knowledge than he had when he was your age. Perhaps you think there's no use trying to think of anything new, that everything's been done. Wrong. The simple, agrarian man of Franklin's day didn't begin to need the answers we need today. What can you do about it? To start with, make a copy of the accomplishments of Benjamin Franklin and read it on your birthday every year until you are eighty-four. Ask yourself if indolence or ingenuity characterizes your life.

New Home, New Records

As I was checking in for my flight from Seattle to Portland recently, I saw what's becoming a more and more familiar sight—immigrants. I could tell they were from Eastern Europe, gathering for a picture of their arrival in their new home—*America*. After I was settled into my seat and had buckled up, I mentioned something to the steward about this, and asked him if he knew where they were from. He told me they were from Hungary, Romania and Russia.

He said, "Every night for the last four years this flight from New York to Seattle and on to Portland has had passengers from Eastern Europe."

"Wow," I said, "America still is the promised land, isn't it?" When I got off the plane, in Portland there was a group waiting for the new arrivals, ready to greet and welcome their European friends and family.

America still is the promised land, though we may take for granted the freedoms, the opportunity to work where we want to work, live where we want to live, go where we want to go, play where we want to play, say what we want to say, and pray where we want to pray.

The experience reawakened me to the opportunity that's all around us. How about you? Have you been "sleep walking?" Are you failing to notice your opportunities to speak and act? Or do you need a wake up call? I've talked to at least four people this week who are exploring new fields, looking for new careers. Many have taken this freedom so for granted, that they have forgotten we can change jobs, earn advancement, change careers, and through greater effort, rise to any heights we're determined to achieve.

Don't wait for someone else to do it first. Consider that, after Roger Banister broke the four-minute mile, 119 others went on to break that barrier and best his record the very same year.

Did these other runners have greater strength, greater ability? I doubt it; once Roger Banister demonstrated to others that it could be done, other runners suddenly had greater belief in their own potential.

Don't underestimate your strengths. The concept of untapped potential *("There lives inside each of us a genius, a power, a capacity—an untapped potential. This possibility for being and becoming is seen in the shadows of our past achievements—the mist of dreams and aspirations. We tap our potential by gaining confidence from our achievements, accepting responsibility for our present and committing to our goals.")* must move from the concept phase to the reality phase. Whose reality? Your reality.

An "old man," Carl Lewis, shattered the record at the Tokyo World's Championships with his 9.86 time for the 100-meter sprint. At the age of 30, he was faster than he ever was in his youth. Burt Reynolds earned his first Emmy after many years of acting. These are both extraordinary accomplishments, outstanding achievements, in fields that require entirely different kinds of talent, knowledge, skills, and ability. Certainly, they both require a similar kind of tenacity, determination, and persistent practice.

You and I may never earn life's "big" prizes: The Pulitzer, the Nobel Peace Prize, an Oscar, an Emmy, or a place in the Guinness Book of World's Records. But, we're all eligible for life's small pleasures: A pat on the back, a four-pound bass, a full moon, an empty parking space, a crackling fire, a great meal, a glorious sunset. And, by applying the same qualities of tenacity, determination, and persistent practice, we can beat our old "personal best," we can achieve distinction in our field.

Today, enjoy the little pleasures life brings. At the same time, redouble your commitment to excellence in your corner of the world, and you, too, can set a new world's record.

"Wait a minute," I can hear you saying. "How can commitment enable me to set a world's record?"

I asked my class, "What is a world's record?" After exploring the classic definition, "the first time it has ever been done," I introduced my Turbo definition: "the first time *you* have ever done it."

If it is the first time you have done something, then it is a world's record for *you*. One of the great ways to experience more of your potential is to make a practice of continually setting world's records by increasing your "first-time-I-have-ever-done-it" incidents. You will stay alive, vibrant and young all of your life.

> *Successful people go beyond necessity to the very limits of possibility because they wonder where those limits lie. Behold, they don't lie anywhere—for like the horizon they expand with every step we take towards them.*
> Cheryl Matschek
> The Cheryl Matschek Company, Portland, Oregon

Want a Raise?

Do you want a raise? It's simple, but not easy or automatic. "Do what you love and the money will follow" may not be wholly true. Just doing what you love may not guarantee that the money will follow because people may not want or be willing to pay for what you produce when you do what you love. For money to follow, you must adhere to three principles:

1. Provide higher *quality* by offering more value or better service than others;

2. Provide greater *quantity* by offering faster service or a lower price than others, or

3. Provide a *unique* service, one that's scarce or in limited supply. Let the law of supply and demand work for *you*. The greater the demand, the less the supply, the higher the price paid.

Be worth more than you are paid. You must be worth more than you are paid if you ever wish to be paid more than you're worth. Most of us look forward to retirement or to working at a more leisurely pace, and we wish to have income in these years—to be paid more than we are worth. There is power in specialized knowledge. Study your area of special interest (what you love) for fifteen minutes a day. Fifteen minutes of study a day, every day, will make you a genius in your chosen field in five years.

Renew your belief in the free-market system and your ability to participate in it. Commit yourself to the three principles for earning a raise. Find a way to provide greater quality of service or a greater quantity of service or a service scarce in the world around you. See yourself participating in the miracle of the free market system. Believe that your efforts will be rewarded and that you *can* successfully participate. As you build your belief, you will experience a sense of personal power and motivation—you will experience the thrust of a turbo-charger.

The law of compensation says that every one gravitates to where they belong in life, just as surely as water seeks and finds its level. Your position is measured precisely by the quality and quantity of the service rendered, plus the mental attitude with which you relate to others. Nothing has yet been invented to take the place of *work.*

When you develop the habit of doing more than you are paid for, you enter an arena where an individual may practice without asking permission; therefore, it is under your control.

By "going the extra mile," you put into action the Golden Rule of doing for others what you'd like done for you. The Golden Rule supplies the right mental attitude while "going the extra mile" supplies the action. Both mental attitude and action are necessary for worthwhile accomplishment.

Wake up to your opportunity! Sit down, *right now*, and list all the possible opportunities that exist in your company, your business, and your community. Then take some decisive action that will help you experience more of your potential.

Opportunity in my company: _____

_____

The extra mile I can go to take advantage of this opportunity:_____

_____

Opportunity in my business: _____

_____

The extra mile I can go to take advantage of this opportunity:_____

_____

Opportunity in my community:_____

_____

The extra mile I can go to take advantage of this opportunity:_____

_____

_____

Be Prepared for Opportunities

Early Saturday morning I watched and scored sales presentations of the professional sales people attending our Turbo Sales Lab. These championship sales talks were ten minutes long. We scored them on twenty-one different, specific steps of the presentation.

I've been training sales people professionally for over twenty-five years, and have always included in this training the expectation that successful completion of the program required a satisfactory, planned sales presentation. So what was different this time? I'd been working with this company and their salespeople a full quarter, once a year, for the past three years. Their progress was truly amazing! The presentations were fluid, lucid, clean, and smooth. The salespeople were confident and professional; even those who were new to the company had risen to the high level established by the senior sales force.

Disciplined learning requires proper preparation and results in confident performance. Take the time to learn your lines, prepare, study, discipline yourself to master your craft, and you'll approach your work with the same fluid, lucid clarity and confidence.

Last week, Ken called to say he'd taken on the responsibility for establishing and organizing a regional distribution center. I first met Ken in the Leadership Lab about five years ago and have observed extraordinary growth in him over the last sixty months. Like Abraham Lincoln, Ken says, "I'll prepare myself, and when my opportunity comes, I'll be ready." The payoff for Ken: raises in pay, greater responsibility, and, most important, a sense of pride, a sense of achievement, a sense of self-direction. Outsiders may see these increases for Ken and say, "He's been lucky." But, what is "luck" anyway? Luck is when opportunity and preparedness meet.

A lesson you can learn from Ken is to make sure you're doing something, today, to honestly and legitimately prepare yourself for the opportunities which are all around. Many of us don't need a better job, we need to be good enough for the job we already have.

Find a meaningful way to do something, today, to prepare yourself for the opportunities that are even now knocking on your door. Make your own luck. That's the turbo-charged way.

Rehearsing

When I arrived in Seattle, late Thursday afternoon, my associate, Roberta, said, "We've got some major problems with our promotion sponsor. She called and raised several objections to our plan—the plan we've already agreed on." Roberta didn't know how to handle her objections, questions, or concerns and had arranged a 7:30 a.m. breakfast for us the following morning. I was preparing to teach a class and had too much on my mind to concern myself with the sponsor's problems. Besides, what could I do?

Before the breakfast meeting on Friday morning, I took a moment to mentally prepare myself for the meeting. "Whatever happens is going to be the best possible arrangement that could possibly happen between us," I told myself. Taking W. Clement Stone's advice, I rehearsed saying, "That's good about the problems arising." I followed the action that Maxwell Mault's recommends in his book *Psycho Cybernetics* by mentally out-picturing, mentally rehearsing the breakfast meeting. I saw exactly what I would say; I saw exactly what she would say; and I saw exactly how the meeting would go. And, more importantly, I saw the outcome of the meeting.

It was a marvelous meeting. We reviewed our projects and our roles, clarified goals, and recommitted to our vision. The upshot was, we were asked to do more billable work, with everyone totally recommitted to the project.

The lesson I learned is the importance of mentally rehearsing before going into any situation, particularly any difficult situation. Instead of worrying about the outcome of an important meeting, mentally rehearse with positive images. You'll have more successes and greater peace of mind.

Recently, Donna Lee and I somewhat begrudgingly (we were hosts just last year), prepared to be banquet hosts once again. When we showed up for a rehearsal, along with about 300 others, we heard an overview of the event and our part in it. We watched a "right way/wrong way" skit intended to reinforce the importance of our role and how to handle each part of a job. Then, we role-played greeting, meeting, and seating guests, followed by questions and answers and a final explanation.

At the time I felt like the elaborate rehearsal was overkill. Reflecting on the successful experience afterward, I'm certain that the event, which was attended by over 1,500 people, was successful because of the preparation that went into assuring its seamless fluidity. I felt more confident about my role, and felt pride in the organization that took the time and trouble to make sure everything proceeded according to plan.

What I learned from the experience is the necessity of taking the time to rehearse for the important events in life. What will you be doing today or this week that's important, that may require a bit of coordination? Take a few minutes to dress-rehearse, to plan it out, and to role-play. I guarantee that if you do, you'll move into the day, the week, and the event, with a greater sense of confidence, pride, and enthusiasm. You'll feel better about yourself, and better about the results. You'll put your best foot forward. You'll be turbo-charged.

> *If you empty your purse into your head, no man can take*
> *it away from you.* —Ben Franklin

Performing

A few years ago I watched in amazed amusement as the old man of tennis, Jimmy Conners, the 174th-ranked player in the U.S. Open, came back and beat the tenth-ranked player. The fans had left the stadium; they'd given up on Conners, but Conners went on to win the U.S. Open on his thirty-ninth birthday.

Youth is a state of mind. I've known people who are old at twelve, and others who were young at ninety. We can overcome the odds if we put our heart into what we do. Today, play with reckless abandon, put your heart into what you do, don't worry about the odds or the fans in the bleachers. Give it everything you have, and you'll be a winner. You owe it to yourself to be exceedingly good at something. What's your pleasure?

> *Many people think that by hoarding money they are*
> *gaining safety for themselves. If money is your only*
> *hope for independence, you will never have it. The only*
> *real security that a person can have in this world is a*

reserve of knowledge, experience and ability. Without these qualities, money is practically useless.

—Henry Ford

The truth is, you have extraordinary potential! Now you need to wake up to your capacity for greatness. Many people cheat themselves out of a rewarding life because they refuse to open themselves to this awareness. They never rise above mediocrity because they fail to acknowledge a fundamental truth: *Each of us harbors the ingredients of success.*

Meeting the Challenge of Change

It's the most unhappy people who must fear change.

—Mignon McLaughin

Heraclitus observed that "No one steps into the same river twice." Twenty-five centuries later, thinkers are still rediscovering the inescapable reality of change. Life and the world keep flowing and evolving.

When I graduated, I moved to Cleveland, Ohio, leaving behind my friends, family, and acquaintances. Going from a small town of 30,000 to a community of three million was quite a shock. I was fortunate to find new friends in a small church that I began attending. It was a neighborhood church that had been founded by German immigrants a generation earlier. One of the founding families attended all the services, Sunday both morning and night, and again on Wednesday nights. The patriarch of the family *always sat in the same seat.* He was getting up in years and had a little palsy which caused his right foot to move back and forth all the time. As the years went by, he had literally worn a groove, a rut, in the hardwood floor of the church. How easy it is for us to find ourselves sitting in the same place, going to the same places, and literally living in a rut, resisting change of any kind. A rut, of course is just a grave with both ends knocked out.

If you can't change your mind are you still sure you have one?

—Bumper sticker

16

Resisting Change

A few years ago while producing a series of training videos, I visited our production company's headquarters. A few days earlier I had parked nearby without adequately feeding the parking meter and had experienced the predictable consequence: a $12 ticket. I was not about to repeat my mistake, but when I parked my car and checked my pockets, I found I had no change. I ran into the bakery across the street, and I asked for change for a dollar.

The clerk said, "We don't make change here. If you want change, you'll have to go down the street two blocks to the bank." I ran down the street to the bank, got two dollars worth of change, ran back to my car, fed the meter, went back into the bakery and asked for the owner. When she came out I gave her a dollar's worth of change and asked her to give it to anyone who asked for parking meter change in the future.

The bakery clerk was a person who resisted "change." Well, that pun aside, most of us are resistant to change. Change generally forces us out of our comfort zones, and when we stand on the cusp on our comfort zone and peer out into the unknown, we experience fear. It's really quite natural. Whether these fears work for us or against us depends upon the choices we make. And these choices determine the quality of our lives. The choices we make about leaving our comfort zone determine whether we stagnate, grow, retreat, really live, or lead lives, as Thoreau says, of quiet desperation.

> *I eat change for breakfast*
> —Phil Knight, President of Nike

We all would like the world to be a better place, and it can be, but only if *we change*. All change isn't better, but there is no "better" without change.

Ask yourself these questions:

Are changes taking place in your community? _____

Describe the changes: _____

_____

_____

Are changes taking place in your business? _____

Describe the changes: _____

_____

_____

Are changes taking place in your personal life? _____

Describe the changes: _____

_____

_____

Change is the order of the day. Change is the only thing that is constant in our world. There is one major difference in change today as compared to change ten or twenty years ago, and that is the *rate* of change. Today things are changing faster than ever, and changes are going to keep coming faster and faster. We are living in an age of "knowledge explosion." The world has doubled its bulk knowledge in the past ten years. We took the accumulated knowledge of about five thousand years of information and doubled that in a tiny fraction of that time. What's mind-boggling is that we are going to double the double in the next ten years. In technical fields we will double that double in five years, half the time.

"Change is inevitable. Growth is optional."

To live happy, fulfilled, turbo-charged lives we must be able to successfully manage change. We must do more than manage change. We must, as Tom Peters says in his book, *Thriving on Chaos*, "Learn to love change." Twenty years ago IBM had no competition. Then a big change took place. Apple Computers entered the market and changed the way everyone sold, bought, and thought about computers forever. Think about it: "Change is inevitable. Growth is optional."

In *The Survivor Personality*, Dr. Al Siebert wrote, "Change requires learning." And:

> People with survivor personalities are ideally suited for a world of constant change because they are always learning how to be better at what they do.

People in the past were raised to have personalities that made them acceptable in a stable, unchanging world. That is why they do not cope well when their job skills or their occupation becomes obsolete. Life's best survivors thrive during times of change because they react to such changes as job loss, divorce, illness, or new technology by asking questions, imagining new and creative ways of doing things, and looking for different ways to be useful—just as they do in their everyday lives...

Like it or not, we are living in a time when change is something you can count on. No matter who you are, or what your profession or business, you can expect that to survive and thrive in the years ahead you will be required to learn and change.

A couple of weeks ago, before making a presentation on Team Management to the Construction Specifications Institute (CSI), I sat across the dinner table from several architects. We were talking about Computer-Aided Design (CAD), a computer program for architects. I asked how many years CAD had been in use. After a brief discussion, I learned CAD had been around for about ten years.

It has been in more common use in just the last three years—another example of break-through technology like that made by FAX machines, E-Mail, and cellular phones. Someone mentioned there's a greater concentration of CAD programs in the Portland area than anywhere else in the Northwest. I mentioned my experience with a Virtual Reality computer program than enables you, with a hood, special gloves and boots, to get a sense of walking down a hall; a sense of space and proportion. The response of the architect sitting across from me was, "Well, I'm ready to retire."

What resistance to change he manifested! I'm a novice when it comes to architectural renderings, but it appears to me that using a CAD program is a far more efficient, effective way of designing than the old T-square and drawing board I learned drafting with, and yet instead of embracing change this architect responded, "I want to retire."

I wanted to say to him, "You already have."

Live In the Present

My son Larry and I made a sales call to a large fruit grower and packing company in Yakima, Washington. We were visiting with one of the third generation owner/managers when her father walked in. She introduced us as management consultants and trainers. The first words out of his mouth were, "I'm an Ivy League graduate and I hate the way the Japanese do business." It seems he hated the Japanese period. After we left their office, my son and I agreed, "There is someone living in the past, unwilling to change."

Today our competition isn't down the street or across town. Our competition is around the world. Individuals and companies today must think globally. If we are going to ignore the Japanese or any of our competitors, we will not make it. Our world has shrunk to the size of a golf ball. The Concorde can fly us from New York to London in three hours. We can FAX a letter from Phoenix to Frankfurt in five minutes.

Robert J. Lifton, a pioneer in the field of psychohistory, the study of relationships between historical events and human behaviors, and a distinguished professor of psychiatry and psychology at the City University in New York says, in his book, *The Protean Self:*

> The fragmentation, dislocation and uncertainties of the modern world have led to a new human capacity for change. Our lives become a balancing act between constancy and search, stability and change. Our protean potential enables us always to re-think and change course. My research suggests that we are ever-capable of fresh insights and larger notions of who we are.

Habit freezes us at our current level of competence. Too often, we don't care if innovation makes for improvement—that doesn't seem to be the issue. Instead, we wonder, "Do I have to learn something new? Is it different? So what if it's easier or faster, do I have to start all over again in understanding how to do my job?" If you think that way, you've already retired.

I don't know how anyone can resist the allure of change. In embracing change, we grow, stay alive, young and alert. Look for ways to change. Embrace a new technology, a new idea, a new behavior, a new attitude. Give up a prejudice, change a paradigm. You'll stay young all your life. You'll be young-at-heart, and people who are young-at-heart live *all* their lives. I recently read this headline in an ad in *The Wall Street Journal*:

> *Malcolm Forbes learned to ride a motorcycle when he was 50.*
>
> —*What have YOU learned lately?*

It's a good question, don't you think? Let's respond to it. Don't wait for change to happen to you. Be the proactive, turbo-charged leader who makes change happen *for* you.

What changes that you resisted during the past ten years turned out for the best? _____

_____

During the past five years? _____

_____

During the past year?_____

_____

During the past month? _____

_____

Today? _____

_____

What changes are you currently resisting? _____

_____

_____

What changes would you like to see take place in your career or personal life? _____

_____

_____

What can you do to prepare for those changes? _____

_____

_____

Chapter 2

Fears and Achievements

"This possibility for being and becoming is seen in the shadows of our past achievements ..."

You've failed many times, although you may not remember. You fell down the first time you tried to walk. You almost drowned the first time you tried to swim, didn't you?

Did you hit the ball the first time you swung a bat? Heavy hitters, the ones who hit the most home runs, also strike out a lot. R. H. Macy failed seven times before his store in New York caught on. English novelist John Creasey got 753 rejection slips before he published 564 books. Babe Ruth struck out 1,330 times, but he also hit 714 home runs.

Don't worry about failure.

Worry about the chances you miss when you don't even try. How high would your goals be if you weren't afraid of failure?

—A message published in the *Wall Street Journal* by United
Technologies Corp. of Hartford, Connecticut

The television program, *The Wide World of Sports*, invited viewers to witness "The thrill of victory and the agony of defeat." Skiers would come down the slope, crash and tumble head over skies; drivers at the Indianapolis race would crash their cars against the wall. Experiencing the thrill of victory is impossible unless you are willing to risk the agony of defeat. You have to strap on the skies, fire up the engine, if you are ever going to live a turbo-charged life.

> *It is not death that a man should fear, but he should fear never beginning to live.*
>
> —Marcus Aurelius

"The only thing we have to fear is fear itself," Roosevelt said in his First Inaugural Address in 1933, echoing the Duke of Wellington whom the Earl of Stanhope quoted as having said, "The only thing I am afraid of is fear." Wellington, in turn, may have been paraphrasing Henry David Thoreau, who said, "Nothing is so much to be feared as fear." And Thoreau may have borrowed the thought from Francis Bacon who, in 1623, wrote, "Nothing is terrible except fear itself." There is also the possibility that Thoreau might have read Michel Montaigne's essay (published in 1580) in which he wrote, "the thing I fear most is fear." But, leave it to the Old Testament to scoop them all: "Be not afraid of sudden fear" (Proverbs 3:25).

"It is fear that holds us back," Shakespeare said. "Our doubts are traitors and make us lose the good we oft might win by fearing to attempt" *(Measure for Measure)*.

The Comfort Zone

All growth and meaningful change occur outside our comfort zone. Are you familiar with Hazel Stout? Born four months before the Wright brothers flew the first airplane, Hazel jumped from an airplane at 10,500 feet in the air to celebrate her 88th birthday. This was just another in Hazel's list of comfort zone expanding experiences over the past 14 years since her husband, Waldo, died. Her achievement unofficially qualifies Hazel for the Guinness Book of World's Records. Hazel was encouraged by her granddaughter and was harnessed to her son-in-law when she jumped. We need the loving support of others when we take big leaps.

When I jumped from an airplane in 1983, I was joined by a few friends. After about four or five hours of training at the Sheridan airport, training that included some theory, a few concepts, and a lot of practice for skill, the jump master asked me to put on my jumpsuit and parachute. As I followed his direction I noticed my heart was beating a little faster and my pulse rate was speeding up. As I walked across the runway toward the dirty, little single-engine, half-worn-out airplane, my heart really began to pound. The plane's paint was dull and all scratched up, the fuselage was covered with oil. Inside, the plane had been gutted, there were no seats, so we sat on the floor. It was *not* a pretty sight.

After we piled into the plane, the pilot started the engine. The *sputter, sputter, cough, cough,* did nothing to strengthen my confidence one iota. As the airplane rattled and bumped down the runway, my confidence was not bolstered. When we reached 4200 feet the pilot idled the engine. For a moment, all I could hear was the silent whisper of the aircraft cutting through the quiet sky. Then the jump master opened the door. Have you ever been in an airplane going 100 mph at 4200 feet in the air, with the door suddenly opened? The rush of noise, and roar of wind fills the inside of the airplane.

The jump master signaled me to exit the aircraft, "Time to jump," he said.

I thought, "Why do I always have to go first?" I weighed more than the others who were waiting to jump. I guess that meant that I would make a bigger splat.

I struggled to reach the foot peg, my pant legs flapping and making a turbulent, roaring sound. I gripped the strut with all my strength. I guess I figured that I could hang on until we landed. My hands slipped, though, and away I went. I was, as you can tell, *way* out of my comfort zone.

My driving experience, on the other hand, has been in my comfort zone and is hardly memorable. I did a little calculating the other day, and I estimate that I have driven almost a million miles: 102,000 in my red '65 Comet Convertible, 80,000 in my white '67 Dodge Charger, 70,000 in my black '70 T-Bird, 94,000 in my baby-blue '72 Chrysler New Yorker; I put 87,000 miles on my 1975 bronze Olds Toronado; then there was the 74,000 miles in my midnight blue '76 Jaguar XJS, followed by 125,000 in the blue '77 Cadillac Seville, 160,000 in the '78 silver Porsche 911SC, 120,000 in the maroon '81 Mercedes 300SD; and our 1986 royal blue Mercedes 300E now reads 101,000. Yet, I cannot tell you in vivid detail about more than a few hundred of all those million miles.

But I sure can tell you in vivid detail about that 4,200 foot drop! I was *alive*. I wasn't sure I would be in another four-and-a-half minutes, but I've never felt more alive than when I glided down through the air from that rickety plane.

Now, I'm not suggesting that you jump out of an airplane. What I am suggesting is that you jump out of your comfort zone. Run for your life. Face your psychological fears—hit them head on. I promise you will enjoy the experience, and you will feel alive.

Our business in life is not to get ahead of others, but to get ahead of ourselves—to break our own records, to outstrip our yesterday by our today.

—Stewart B. Johnson

Years ago, in one of my classes, a student told the story of a bully who chased her home after school each day, teasing her, pulling her pigtails, and generally terrorizing her. She suffered from asthma, and one day when the bully was chasing her up a long hill she ran out of air. She simply couldn't run any farther. So she stopped, turned around, and looked him straight in the eyes. When she did that he backed down, and ran the other way! So it is with our fears. If we face them they tend to turn and run the other way. This is among the first steps to living a turbo-charged life.

Take a look at your own life. What were your most exhilarating experiences? List those high points, those mountain peak experiences, those times when you were most alive, most fulfilled. What risks did you have to take?

I was turbo-charged when: _____

_____

_____

_____

I had to risk _____

_____

_____

Most of the things you have included on your "turbo-charged" list were outside of your comfort zone. The joy and thrill of living is not staying in our comfort zones looking for maximum security, but venturing out—looking for maximum growth.

*There is a tide in the lives of men, which, when taken at
the flood leads to victory.* —William Shakespeare

Confronting Your Fears

In 1492, Columbus confronted society's fears, and the world was
changed forever. Talk about stepping out of your comfort zone! Columbus jumped out—dove out of his comfort zone. Certainly, there
were nay-sayers of the time who felt the world was flat, but he alone
had the courage of his convictions, the tenacity to act on his beliefs,
to stand against conventional wisdom, to put himself on the line. He
withstood real and imagined criticism and ridicule. He changed the
world, but first he changed his mind and the mind of others. He had
the courage of his convictions, and he sailed through his fears and
the fears of the "group-think" of the fifteenth century.

Now, look at the assumptions you make about what frightens
you. Maybe, one of the fears you've bought based on the "group-
think" of your society is of questionable validity. Jump out of your
comfort zone, sail through your fear. You'll discover new worlds
for yourself, and since others are always watching, you'll chart a
new path for others to follow—and that's leadership.

*Every ship that comes to America gets its chart from
Columbus.* —Ralph Waldo Emerson

The subconscious mind plays a large role in fear, especially fear
of change. We store reactions to fear in our subconscious minds and
the fears create undesirable situations for us in our daily lives. Perhaps the most common fear we have is the fear of separation, aban-
donment and isolation. A child who has been momentarily lost in a
department store may retain this experience as terrifying. Long after
the experience has been consciously forgotten, the child may have
extremely fearful reactions to simple situations, and cling to the
wrong people later in life.

It's never too late to do something definite about your fears if
you are willing to face them, understand them, and work through
them. Attack your fears in an enthusiastic, adventurous way. You
will benefit greatly, not only in your own life, but also in your relationships because you will understand others better. You'll know
that others have fears, from the top executive to the cleaning person,

and you'll relate to others with greater tolerance and with greater understanding.

Find a "buddy" who will support, challenge, motivate, and hold you accountable to what you commit to do to expand your comfort zone. Find a "cheerleader" to cheer you on, a friend who will help you strengthen your commitment and give you additional courage to stand up to your fears.

Answer truthfully:

What are you afraid of?_____

_____

I have asked this question of audiences across the United States and in seven countries around the world. The answer I have heard most often is "the unknown." However, we are not really afraid of the unknown; we are afraid of what we *associate* with the unknown; and what we generally associate with it is an inability to cope; that is, *failure*.

And, why are we afraid of failure?

Most of us are afraid of the loss of comfort, security, love, respect, power, admiration, and affection. What are you afraid of losing?

Take the time to answer that question right now.

I am afraid of losing _____

_____

_____

Now ask yourself, "What might I gain if I weren't afraid of this?"

I might gain _____

_____

Behind all indecision is fear, fear of loss. Listing your fears can be a great first step in facing your fears and facing your fears will put them on the run. Fear is a coward and a bully. If you let it, it will push you around, and you will never own your own power. I challenge you to *stand up, speak out, and be counted*. Take a stand, and face your fears head on.

If you do things you are afraid of doing, the death of fear is certain.   —Ralph Waldo Emerson

It's always exciting when we kick off another Leadership Lab. At the end of the evening, I asked everyone in attendance how they benefited from the session, what their learning experience had been. Charlie said, "I stood up, in front of the group, made a talk, and survived." This was, for Charlie, an exhilarating, empowering, stimulating experience.

What can we learn from Charlie's experience? By identifying a fear, admitting it, resolving to face it, acting upon it, moving through it, and standing against it, we'll have the personal discovery of learning that we do survive. Yes, *we* survive, but the fear dies. Fear is dispelled by action, and positive, self-directed action is the most certain way to dispel fear.

What a sense of exhilaration you'll experience when you face your fears and act upon them. They will disappear, and new-found confidence and excitement will be yours, and it will see you through your next challenge.

Are you in earnest, seize this very minute. Whatever you can do, or think you can, begin it. Boldness has genius, power and magic in it. Only engage, and then the mind grows heated. Begin it and the work will be completed.
                    —Johann von Goethe

Seize the opportunity to *do something* about your fears and overcome them. Recognize the fear for what it is, and develop a plan to make that fear work for you. Take little steps, but be sure you take them. Think about your fears for a moment. Inventory the fears in the different areas of your life and ask yourself:

If I were not afraid, what would I be doing about my career, my

finances, my health, and my personal life?_____

_____

_____

_____

The fear I want to conquer now is: _____

_____

My plan of action to overcome this fear is:_____

_____

_____

Three things that are out of my psychological comfort zone that I will do this week: _____

_____

_____

We are constantly radiating something to those around us. We can radiate doubt, fear, anxiety *or* trust, hope, faith and courage.

If you're looking for security I can tell you where to find it: in a state prison. In fact, if you act in a certain manner they'll put you in a place called maximum security. They'll feed you, house you, and clothe you.

If that doesn't sound inviting, consider that staying in your comfort zone is just like being in a prison cell. The walls get thicker and higher, and it's almost impossible to escape. Wouldn't you rather make a lifestyle of courageously exploring the space beyond your comfort zone?

If you succumb to the temptation of remaining in your comfort zone in the pursuit of security, you will eventually become bored. Yours will be a life that lacks zest, vim and vigor, a life that's as flat as a bottle of 7-Up that's been left in the refrigerator with the cap off. At first, you'll say, "My life is so boring."

Beneath boredom lies depression. Our society is experiencing depression in epidemic proportions. Much depression is self-imposed and comes as a result of a rigid withdrawal from life—retreating, instead of advancing—going backwards instead of marching forward into life.

> *Do what you're afraid to do. When you run away because you are afraid to do something big, you pass opportunity by.*   —W. Clement Stone

Overcoming Your Limitations

I talked to a fellow who was enrolled in our Leadership Lab last week. He had not shown up for Session Two of the program, telling us that he had something previously scheduled. Then he called between Session Two and Three to tell us he wasn't going to come back to the class. He said he wasn't returning to the class, because he would have to speak before the group. This was the real reason he didn't come to Session Two; he found out his assignment was to make a two-minute talk in front of the class.

He said he was uncomfortable speaking in front of groups. He said, "I've always been this way, and I'm not going to start changing now." The fact that he was uncomfortable in front of groups didn't come as a surprise to me. I've coached thousands of people who were petrified to speak in front of a group; some broke down and cried, trembled, even lost control of bodily functions. These same people, after just a few sessions, were laughing with their audience and moving and speaking with confidence and grace.

When I hear people say, "I haven't done it before, and I'm not about to start now," I can almost hear them saying, "I'm staying exactly where I am; I'm not moving forward with my life. If I haven't done it up until now, if I haven't faced and conquered my fears, I am not going to start now." What a dogmatic declaration of limitation, what a great way to keep marching in place, going in circles—digging a rut for yourself. And, as you recall, a rut is just a grave with both ends knocked out.

Argue for your limitations and sure enough they are
yours. — Jonathan Livingston Seagull

Take Risks

Diane, one of our MasterMind partners, enjoyed Thanksgiving with her 98-year-old grandmother. Diane's grandmother was in her thirties throughout the Great Depression; she saw the automobile developed, air-travel become common, radio and television invented. She doesn't find innovation commonplace, though; she appreciates new developments that improve upon our lives, because she can remember what it was like without modern conveniences. In all Diane's excited talk about her grandmother, I could tell that her grandmother is definitely one of the "young olds."

In 1991, Stanford reported the results of an eighteen-year study of what they called the "young olds": people who have reached what is commonly referred to as "old age" but who are youthful in appearance, health, demeanor and brightness.

In 1513, Ponce de Leon, the Spanish explorer, drank water from a spring on a peninsula of the North American coast, which he called Florida (meaning "covered with flowers"), hoping he'd discovered the Fountain of Youth. Some people are still looking for that fountain of youth. Do you remember the old Geritol ads? They promised rejuvenation, invigoration, stimulation—an elixir of youth. But you can't buy youth any more than you can buy a mental attitude.

The "young olds" seem to have drunk from the fountain of youth, but what they've really ingested is a youthful attitude. Stanford's research revealed that what will keep you alive all of your life, what will help you be one of the "young olds" instead of one of the "old youngs" are three attitudes.

The first is pure optimism—the determination to see opportunities in difficulties. Albert Hubbard said, "Optimism is a kind of heart stimulant—the digitalis of failure." Optimism is characterized by *cheerfulness,* which is a happy, warm, positive attitude; by *expectancy,* which enables the optimist to look forward instead of backward; and by *hopefulness,* which is a belief in a better day. Hope colors everything with a broad, bright hue. Color your life with the broad brush of optimism. Drink the elixir of optimism, see through the rose-colored glasses of optimism, and you'll be young all of your life.

Attitude number two of the "young olds" is an attitude of forgiveness. They seem to have even developed the ability to be thankful for trials, difficulties and challenges. Pure optimism is the attitude of gratitude. Researchers concluded that the cells of our body respond, dance with delight, to the music of gratitude. To practice forgiveness unloads our burdens, makes us lighter.

If you would like to lose some weight real fast, just forgive and accept forgiveness. The lightness you receive when you release grudges that you might hold, when you forgive, will make you young all of your life.

Guess what the third attitude to life is that the Stanford study noted? The "young olds" are risk takers! They are willing to try the new, the unusual; they're willing to take chances—to jump out of their comfort zone, to push the envelope.

These three attributes, *optimism, forgiveness,* and *risk-taking,* will help you keep young all of your life. They will help you be one of the "young olds."

There's no better day for you to embrace these three attitudes of optimism, forgiveness and risk-taking than today. What do you have to lose besides boredom and placid complacency? What do you have to gain? For starters, the ability to become one of the "young olds." You can be young all of your life and, in the process, you will be turbo-charged.

Break Through Walls

As we drove north from our son's place in Long Beach, California, (a subdued coastal town with magnificent homes looking out over boardwalks toward the ocean), I noticed that our gas warning light was on. We had been distracted by the complexity of the freeway interchanges, but now I grew concerned. We exited I-5 at Fourth Street in Los Angeles and were suddenly in a different world. Graffiti was everywhere, most signs were in a different language—not twenty minutes from familiar surroundings, but from all appearances we were in a different world.

We found a gas station, filled the tank, got back on the expressway, and continued north, through Hollywood and Universal Studios—a world of glitter, Rolls-Royces, opulence. What separates these worlds? Certainly not vast distances or an ocean. Education perhaps, expectations possibly, roots maybe, networks possibly, opportunity maybe. This is a free society. There are no forced ghettos.

No one is required by law to live in certain limited, literally walled-in, areas. Can people leave these areas and go from Hollywood to being broke? Can a person go from the inner city to the posh suburbs? It happens every day, but most of us never leave the strata we are born into.

What will you do to dramatically explore more of your potential?

What will you do that you haven't done before? What wall, what barriers can you break through—*will* you break through? This is the time to leave behind self-imposed limitations. When you do so, it will enable you to rise to new heights, to be turbo-charged.

Remove Your Mask

Last fall, I saw kids waiting at the bus stop wearing wonderful Halloween costumes. There were coneheads, ghosts, cheerleaders, witches, goblins, masks of all kinds. It reminded me of a Leadership Lab graduation years earlier.

Laurel, the executive assistant to the president of a firm that employs 20,000 people throughout the Northwest, was the moderator. Eight class members walked up on the stage with the most wonderfully decorated brown paper bags over their heads that I've ever seen. They had earrings dangling down, wild hair, huge, beautiful, red lips, great big fake eyelashes.

Laurel said, "When we started the Leadership Lab, we discovered we were all wearing masks, and, as the class progressed, we were able to remove them." As she said this, the class members pulled their brown paper bags off their heads. "And we discovered," she went on to say, "that under our masks we had masks." To my amazement, the class members who uncovered themselves had on big, Groucho Marx horn-rimmed glasses with giant noses and black mustaches. "Ultimately," Laurel said, "we were able to remove all the masks."

Jann Mitchell, in "Relating," her Sunday column in the *Oregonian,* wrote a wonderful editorial in which she spelled out her version of the masks we all wear, most of us on occasion, some of us year 'round. "Instead of being vulnerable," she said, "many of us hide behind facades that keep us from feeling less than perfect."

> These masks include "The Joker" (we make a joke out of anything and everything); "The Sexpot" or "Super Stud" (our dress is sexually flamboyant and our talk is too); "Lookin' Good" (our rent's past due, our teenager's on drugs, but we are always "fine"); "Mr. or Ms. Efficiency" (we zip around getting everything done, that way we don't have the time to look at what's bothering

34

us); "Poor Little Me" (we will list our litany of complaints to anyone; as long as we are the victim, we'll never have to take responsibility for the fix we are in); "Mr. or Mrs. Superior" (our house, car, vacation, children, job and even our gas mileage are always better than yours.)

Do you spot your costume here? Let's throw out these outmoded masks. Being a whole, human, vulnerable and imperfect person is so much easier.

If you are going out tonight, have a ball, have a wonderful time. Put on the greatest costume of your life, let your hair down, have an incredibly wonderful time. And, when you come home, take off your mask, your makeup, set aside your costume. As you're doing so, set aside any of the other masks you may have been wearing on a daily basis.

As you set aside these masks, your desire to be open, vulnerable and real will show through. You will have greater creative spontaneity; the real you will step forward. You'll be lighter, you'll be joyous. You will be turbo-charged.

Take Stock of Yourself

Earlier we took an inventory of our fears. Looking at your successes, the victories in your life will help you defeat your fears and expand your comfort zone. Success isn't measured in how high you climb, but rather in the number of obstacles you've overcome. Stop being your own worst critic. Comparing yourself to others can lead to complacency or cynicism.

You will always be performing at higher levels than many you went to school with, grew up or hung out with. There will also always be people who are achieving above your performance level. There may be many who seem to get on effortlessly, and succeed in spite of many shortcomings and foibles.

One of the great tragedies of the average person's life is disassociation and vicarious living, vicarious success. They live through soap opera characters, television or movie stars, favorite athletes, teams, political figures, children, grandchildren or friends, instead of recognizing and celebrating their own successes.

Low self-esteem can easily be seen in our tendency to disassociate from compliments. We owe it to ourselves to acknowledge *our* achievements, *our* accomplishments. We are not undeserving of compliments. When you are complimented, accept it with thanks.

On the *long*, 12-hour drive back to Oregon from Lake Tahoe, California, we detoured from the expressway, took Highway 20 through the Sierra Mountains, which is a beautiful drive through gold rush country, and then Highway 99, through what looks to be the world's headquarters for English walnuts and almonds. As we drove, we reviewed our two-week vacation—snapshots, Technicolor stereo memories, mostly of our time with our five-year old granddaughter. A full, rich life is a vital mixture of living full out toward meaningful goals and the accumulation of vital, vivid memories.

New Year's Eve we went to a great dance at the Convention Center. There must have been 1,000 people there. There was no alcohol; there was no smoking. The only problem was, you could hardly get on the dance floor. The band called Panama was hot, unbelievably versatile. Carl, a friend of ours, was dressed in tails. He told me it was the first time in his life he'd worn a tux. Everyone looked so handsome. We danced like kids. When we got home, we were so excited, we could hardly go to sleep. We finally turned out the lights, and then I began to feel the aches, but they were good aches.

What I learned from this experience is the importance of *celebrating*, learning how to get high on life. Celebrate with energy, involvement. Go full out. Rent a tux. Get high on life. You'll be building positive memories. Getting high on life is one of the best ways to get turbo-charged.

In a talk before the Vancouver City Club, I mentioned that Donna Lee and I had spent the previous Saturday writing in our ledger book the highlights of 1993. Our ledger book contains thirty years of highlights and successes (year after year after year). If our house were to catch on fire, one of the first things we'd save would be our ledger book of memories.

After my presentation, Bob, an advertising executive came up to me and said, "My wife and I are going to the coast, this weekend. I'm going to take along a notebook. I'm going to write down all of our successes of '93, and I'm going to write down our goals for 1994." In so doing, Bob made a decision to spring into action, to act on his idea to review his past. His future confidence will be better for it. He is on his way to being turbo-charged.

Leverage the Past

Recently, Susan talked with me about her goals, what she wants to do, how she plans to do it and, more importantly, how she feels about her goals, what turns her on, motivates, challenges and stimulates her. Susan's a schoolteacher going into professional sales. She'll be calling on top-level executives. She told me that when she first started thinking about this major career change, she wondered if she could enjoy, being "turned on" and successful as a salesperson.

The process Susan went through included reviewing her past successes, the things that she's enjoyed in the past and done well. As she retraced her past, she realized that she had been extremely successful at some summer sales work, in the course of which she'd called on corporate executives. Realizing that this past success required many of the same skills and qualities, she's now enthusiastic, eager and confident.

What about you? What new goals or projects would you like to undertake? Is there anything you are afraid of tackling, anything you're wondering or tentative about?

Here's the secret: Explore your past successes, identify and isolate the source of those successes—the qualities you drew upon. Identifying the source of your successes will give you confidence and enthusiasm as you see the similarities to your present situation. For all goals you set, you will be turbo-charged.

Dust off your trophies. That's what twenty-four Salem-area managers, superintendents, project managers, comptroller, and owners did when they stepped before our Leadership Lab, one at a time, and shared one of their past successes and achievements. I saw plaques, diplomas, certificates, trophies and medals. I heard stories of people who had overcome setbacks, injuries and obstacles and gone on to become winners. As the stories unfolded, I could feel the optimism rise in the room, the esprit-de-corps. It felt like we were all surrounded by winners, eagles, and it's easy to soar when you're surrounded by winners.

Now it's your turn to dust off you past achievements, keeping in the forefront of your mind your accomplishments, achievements, and strengths. Dig around in your closets, look on your back shelves, find some of your trophies, diplomas and medals, remember how it felt when you achieved these accomplishments, as you overcame your obstacles. Recall the sense of accomplishment and achievement that was yours. That sense of achievement and the feeling of strength will give you all the courage you need to face today's challenges, and you'll be turbo-charged.

Pick one of the highlights and look at the strength you drew on to create that success. This effort will give you the courage to face new challenges, the confidence to set higher goals, and *that's* motivation.

To gain real insight into your potential and to experience the burst of power of a turbo-charger, learn to look at your successes as indicators of what is possible for you. That's at the heart of this positive, self-directed processing of your experiences.

Take a few minutes to inventory and describe the highlights of your life up until now (your successes, your vital, vivid memories); this will help you decide what you want to achieve in the year ahead. Remember, *Your strengths are found in the shadows of your past achievements...and the shadows of your achievements, if you understand them, are the strengths you drew upon to accomplish these feats.*

The major achievements of my life thus far are:_____

_____

_____

_____

_____

_____

_____

The achievements of the past year that I am most proud of are:____

_____

_____

_____

_____

_____

Every day is filled with accomplishments and successes, if you have the perception to see them and the confidence to accept them. You don't have to win a gold medal every day. People with depth see success in everyday events, so complete the following sentence:

Today, I have succeeded in: _____

_____

_____

_____

_____

Wherever I go, I carry with me, in my appointment book, a growing list of my past achievements, my successes for the past fifteen years. Whenever I feel discouraged, tempted to quit, I take out my list of past successes to build my confidence.

Stop here, do not read further in this book, until you have listed at least nine important past achievements in your career, finances, family life, academically, physically and in your social life:

1. _____

2. _____

3. _____

4. _____

5. _____

6. _____

7. _____

8. _____

9. _____

What strengths did you draw upon to create each of these successes?

1. _____

2. _____

3. _____

4. _____

5. _____

6. _____

7. _____

8. _____

9. _____

"Too often we write our successes in water and our failures in brass."

Chapter 3

Dreams and Aspirations

"...the mist of our dreams and aspirations..."

If you can see it, if you can imagine it, you can achieve it; God didn't play any tricks on his highest creation.
—Ralph Waldo Emerson

Explore your dreams, your wants, your likes, and your hopes. Look at your "someday" list. As you examine these misty, unframed foggy images, you will discover more of your true potential.This may be your most important work—gathering, collecting, selecting, taking snapshots of your dreams and aspirations.

Most people don't know what they want, but they are pretty sure they do not have it.   —Pogo

Do Be Have

First, bring your dreams into focus. This will help you to clarify and crystallize your goals. Start by singling out some of the people you admire, people who *do* some of the things you would like to *do*, and *act* like the kind of person you would like to *be*. If it's easier to list some of the things we would like to *have*, that's all right, too. Just list everything, and I do mean *everything,* you would like to have. Do not compromise. Remember, for the moment, this is just a dream list. The wonderful thing about the things we want that we do not now *have*, and the things we would like to do that we have not yet done, is that they drive us to our higher goal of *becoming* the kind of person we are capable of *being*.

41

You and I, the person writing and the person reading these lines, will never have a dramatically better job, house or car, we will never lead a turbo-charged life—*never*—until we first *become better*. That does not mean that we should not make a treasure map or a self-image book (more about that later), for we most certainly must compose a vision statement that describes us as the ideal person we wish to become.

To compose a vision statement, first get in touch with your vision and purpose by listing your core beliefs. List at least seven principles that motivate you. Then ask yourself, "Why do I believe this principle?"

1. I believe in _____

   because _____

   _____

2. I believe in _____

   because _____

   _____

3. I believe in _____

   because _____

   _____

4. I believe in _____

   because _____

   _____

5. I believe in _____

   because _____

   _____

6. I believe in _____

   because _____

   _____

7. I believe in _____

   because _____

   _____

Based on these core beliefs, create a magnetic vision describing in graphic detail how you want your perfect future to look. Your vision statement will provide an image of your desired future. This effort will help you discover what you really want to have, and it is essential in tapping your potential and living a fuller, richer, more productive life. This work will unleash your potential to *be* more than you are. It will help you tap your unrealized potential.

> *All men dream but not equally. Those who dream by night in the dusty recesses of their minds wake in the day to find that it was vanity; but the dreamers of the day are dangerous men, for they may act on their dreams with open eyes to make it possible.*
>
> —T. E. Lawrence

Communicate

Recently, I met with Clifton to explore with him his possible role on our team. I've known Clifton for over twelve years. As we talked, Clifton said, in so many words, "Here are my values, how I express these values, time I give to my values, and here's where I am personally, this is what I feel I must do to grow in my work. Can I find a way, on the TMS team, to express and maintain my core values and still have time left over for my outside interests while making a contribution to your team?"

Everyone wants an answer to this question. Everyone wants to know and, at some level, is struggling with this challenge of balance and integrity—this challenge of expressing values. Because of the nature of our work, the intensity of our work, this question always comes up. In Clifton's case, however, it was easier than it usually is to answer the question because Clifton is clear about what his values are, and he can express what his values are.

Clarify your values, your vision, how you wish to express your values, your vision, and how your work contributes to the expression of your values. This exercise will help you restore your drive, your energy, it will build your morale, will give you a greater sense of peace and personal integrity. This sense of peace and personal integrity will help to turbo-charge you.

Don told our Seattle Leadership Lab a story, prefacing it by say-ing, "This is not a sad story." Then, he went on to say, "About a year ago, my brother attempted suicide. I was able to get together with him. We went out to the beach, built a campfire, and stayed there all night talking—just talking. I learned so much about my brother that night that I'd never known, and he learned a great deal about me. We kept up our campfire weekend vigils for several weeks. Out of that came a lot of healing for our entire family. My brother and I still have lunch every other Friday. The lesson I learned is: Out of great pain can come great gain."

Is someone in your world experiencing some pain? If so, go into action, exercise leadership, find a way to have a beachside or fire-side chat. Share your heart, and let that person share his or hers. The healing that occurs will go beyond first appearances. Most of all, perhaps, knowing you've made such a powerful difference will em-power you, and this empowerment will help you be turbo-charged.

While I worked at the office one Saturday morning, Donna Lee was in an all-day seminar. I was head-down, writing, organizing, cleaning up, and planning for the coming week, when the phone rang. It was my wife. "Where are you, you stinker? I thought we'd have lunch together. I have 'til 2:00 before I have to be back at the seminar. I thought you'd be fooling around the garage." I dashed home, and we had a simple salad, but it was the best lunch of the week. It's hard to explain why. We talked, shared, communicated about what was going on in the seminar. We sort of communed to-gether until Donna needed to return to the seminar. I was reminded of the story about a couple who lived in a third-floor apartment. They were in financial difficulties and weren't able to pay the rent. Finally, they were put out. On the way down the stairs (she was car-rying a lamp under one arm and a bird cage under the other—he had a baby and a vacuum cleaner), the wife stopped and began to laugh. Finally, the husband said, "Mary, this is no laughing matter." She answered, "Yes, it is. This is the first time we've gone out together in nine years."

Take time out with the ones you love. Today, stop the music for a moment. Sit down across from the person you love. For just a moment, look them straight in the eye, and ask, "How's it going? What did you learn? What was the highlight?" I guarantee that included in the benefits you'll gain from this will be bonding and a sense of oneness. You'll go out into the world with renewed strength and confidence.

Regrets

One of the ways to arrive at a greater understanding of what you want is to take a look at your regrets. Plato warned that "the unexamined life is not worth living." If you can list your regrets, your "if only's" I can help you determine your goals. For example, if you regret not having gotten your degree, your goal might be to become better-educated, to be more well-read, or to return to school to get your degree. That's a goal. If you regret that your marriage isn't fulfilling, maybe your goal is to have a successful marriage that includes love, mutual trust and respect. If you regret not getting a promotion you wanted, your goal might be to make yourself deserving of the next opportunity for promotion. Of course, it's unhealthy to live in the past. But, if examining your past and your regrets gives you some clues as to what your goals are, it can be a very productive activity.

Now write down some of your regrets:

I wish I had: _____

_____

_____

_____

_____

_____

_____

_____

_____

_____

Leap through space and time. Write it down, talk it out, paint a vivid picture with words. Then, get in touch with the twelve-year-old inside you, the innocent twelve-year-old who believes more fervently than you do, and entrust your vision to that little believer. Let that twelve-year-old take the gift of what you vividly imagine and hold it as if it were real today. Holding this gift in your mind will, in fact, help to turbo-charge you.

What dreams, what goals, are revealed by your regrets list? _____

_____

_____

_____

_____

_____

Buying the Farm

"Ever since my wife and I got married we have wanted to live in the country on a farm," Raleigh told our Leadership Lab. "When we were first married, we lived in town. We then moved to Arizona, to another town where the kids were close to school and friends. And yet we would always dream of having a home in the country where the kids would have a lot of room to roam and play, have some room to raise some animals and learn some new things.

"When we moved back to Oregon, we set a goal to look for a home in the country. At first we rented a house while we were looking for a house to buy, but we never lost site of our goal.

"After looking at approximately 50 homes we found our farm house in the country. We moved into our home on an acre-and-a-half in the Fall of '92. It has been everything that we dreamed of.

"The lesson I learned from this is the importance of dreaming big and then converting that dream to goals and to be persistent in pursuing them until they are achieved."

"Don't lose sight of your dreams. Find the goal that is revealed by your dreams. It may take some time to achieve, but you can reach it if you keep trying. The benefit you will gain is the fulfillment of your heart's desire."

Shared Optimism

I stopped for a bite to eat on my way to making a presentation in Beaverton. I was writing and preparing for a talk, and I dropped a folded page of notes I was discarding on the front counter when I picked up my meal. As I was eating, the seventeen-year-old host approached me. "Is this yours?" he asked.

I told him I was discarding the notes. Half-jokingly I said, "You can read them. I think you might enjoy them."

He came back a few minutes later and said, "Pardon me; I did read what you'd written. I really liked it, especially the part about turning your disadvantages into advantages, turning your scars into stars. What do you do?"

I said, "I'm an author, speaker and consultant. Most important of all, I conduct leadership skills training."

Away he went. Then he came back. He said, "You're Larry Dennis."

I said, "Yes, I am."

He stuck out his hand and said, "I'm James Walker. I loved your book, *Repeat Business*." The stars in his eyes reminded me a little of myself when I was a teenager. The wonder in his face was filled with optimism, possibilities. He had a nothing-can-stop-me air about him. He had the courage to reach out, to be proactive, to interact with me.

You can recapture some of the wonderment, the unstoppable optimism and self-confidence of youth. Regardless of your age, today is the first day of the rest of your life. Why not act like it? You've made some mistakes, and that's good because you've learned from those mistakes, but don't let those lessons steal your joy, your optimism, your fervor, and don't be surprised when someone approaches you and says, "Pardon me, who are you?"

Tap your Talents

Visiting the wonderful downtown Portland arts festival, Artquake, we came across a large crowd of people standing around a singing group. We worked our way to the front of the crowd and were amazed at what we saw. The open guitar box sign said "Like Father Like Daughter." There was Dad, singing and playing the guitar. Lined up on his right like little stair steps were three daughters (they looked to be about ten, eight, and six), with mom singing and holding the baby. They sang with such bravado and animation and enthusiasm, it seemed their whole heart was in what they were doing. The audience loved them, and the guitar box filled up with money.

We all have talents of diverse kinds, many of them hidden. We're at our best when we identify our talents and sing out—whether it's blowing glass, making jewelry, or singing for our supper. Why not find a way today to express one of your many talents? Do it with your family if you can. You'll be amazed at how this creative expression multiplies, spills over into your daily life, gives you a sense of pride, personal power, and motivation.

Dreams

We took the afternoon off to tour the new builder displays of latest styles and innovations, the "Street of Dreams." The state-of-the-art technologies, the beautiful finishes, the breakthrough ideas of these dream homes caused me to wonder who buys these castles priced above the affordable level of most of the folks who tour them? We know that it all begins with a dream—first in the *mind* and the heart of the architect and the builder, in a *dream* in the part of the new owner.

Dream again. Brush off an old ideal. Didn't most of the good you enjoy today start with a dream? Most of us don't need better means, we need bigger dreams. Build some castles in the air today. When you can't dream any longer, you die. Build some castles in the sky, and watch your dreams come true.

Scott, the owner operator of a world-class wood trim and finishing company, stood in front of our Leadership Lab and said, "I was born with a passion for cars. I work to provide for my family and support my addiction to cars. So when I attended a hot rod show in 1965 and saw the star of the show, a custom-made, tubular framed street rod that would do 130 miles an hour in a quarter of a mile, it was no surprise I felt love at first sight. But I was eighteen years old, and $22,000 was a little out of my reach.

"I had some sleepless nights as I fantasized about driving it to a prom. I never forgot the car, had a lot of cars since, but I never forgot it. On October 1, 1991, I attended, as I often do, a local collectors' car auction. There it was. There it was! Not quite so glorious as it was thirty years earlier, but there it was. It's in my car garage now. We—my son and I—have the most exciting winter project to work on together." Scott said, "The lesson I learned is that when I turn my dreams to goals and never lose sight, never forget them, my dreams come true."

Rekindle an old desire, an old dream. Dust it off, roll it out, parade it around, and, before you know it, it will no longer be a dream, it will be parked in your garage.

> *Yesterday is but a dream, tomorrow is but a vision,*
> *But today well lived makes every yesterday*
> *a dream of happiness and every tomorrow*
> *a vision of hope. Look well, therefore, to this day.*
> —Ancient Sanskrit proverb

After a full day of facilitating a partnering session for the Oregon Department of Transportation I went to my hotel room, turned on public T.V., and watched Kenny Rogers' concert from the Fox Theater in Atlanta. How his audience loved him, singing every song along with him, clapping—oh, the genius of the gray fox. Midway through the concert, Kenny said, "When I was twelve years old, I vividly imagined myself at the Fox Theater in Atlanta, singing Bo Diddly." I must say, I wasn't surprised that he'd been able to live his dream. It's not an accident that Kenny's where he is. I know when I was sixteen, I began to vividly imagine myself standing before audiences with influence and impact. And aren't you, today, where you began imagining yourself years ago? What's more, we are even larger than our aspirations, bigger than our dreams.

The lesson to learn is the importance of capturing a picture of what you really want and holding that picture vividly in your mind, rehearsing it with color, shape, feeling. As an example, where would you like to be in December of 2010? Visualize it! It surely will come.

Another way to uncover and discover your dreams is to make a wish list. Our wishes are not goals, but our wishes can help us arrive at an understanding of our true goals.

In the programs I have been leading for twenty-five years, we ask participants to write out their goals—one-year, five-year, ten-year goals. This assignment is one of the most difficult tasks for most people. We really do find it hard to quantify our future. Examine where you have been happiest, felt most fulfilled, look at some of your regrets, and look at the people you admire and would like to be more like.

Before I ask you to write your dream list, read the list John Goddard wrote out as a young boy of fifteen. He was sitting in the family room of his home reading a book when he overheard his older relatives in the next room discussing all the things they would have liked to have done, their "wish I had's." He could tell that they were speaking from the framework of regret. And he thought to himself, "If I don't want to be where they are when I'm an adult, I need to decide what I want to do now, and get busy doing it." John Goddard wrote out 126 goals, and as you can see from the list attached, he was stretching, to say the least.

By the time he was forty-seven, Goddard had reached most of these goals.

John Goddard's Goal List
(Note, an "x" indicates completion)

Explore:
1. Nile River (x)
2. Amazon River (x)
3. Congo River (x)
4. Colorado River (x)
5. Yangtze River, China (x)
6. Niger River
7. Oninoco River, Venezuela
8. Rio Coco, Nicaragua (x)

Study primitive cultures in:
9. The Congo (x)
10. New Guinea (x)
11. The Sudan (x) (nearly buried alive in a sandstorm)
12. Brazil (x)
13. Australia (x)
14. Kenya (x)
15. The Philippines (x)
16. Tanganyika (x) (now Tanzania)

17. Ethiopia (x)
18. Nigeria (x)
19. Alaska (x)

Climb:

20. Mt. Everest
21. Mt. Aconcagua, Argentina
22. Mt. McKinley
23. Mt. Huascaran, Peru (x)
24. Mt. Kilimanjaro (x)
25. Mt. Ararat, Turkey (x)
26. Mt. Kenya (x)
27. Mt. Cook, New Zealand
28. Mt. Popocatepetl, Mexico (x)
29. The Matterhorn (x)
30. Mt. Rainier (x)
31. Mt. Fuji (x)
32. Mt. Vesuvius (x)
33. Mt. Bromo, Java (x)
34. Grand Tetons (x)
35. Mt. Baldy, California (x)

Explore underwater:

36. Great Barrier Reef, Australia (x) (photographed a 300-pound clam)
37. Coral reefs of Florida (x)
38. Red Sea (x)
39. Fiji Islands (x)
40. The Bahamas (x)
41. Okefenokee Swamp and the Everglades (x)

Visit:

42. North and South Poles
43. Great Wall of China
44. Panama and Suez Canals (x)
45. Easter Island
46. The Galapagos Islands
47. Vatican City (x) (saw The Pope)
48. The Taj Mahal (x)
49. The Eiffel Tower (x)
50. The Blue Grotto, Capri (x)
51. The Tower of London (x)
52. The Leaning Tower of Pisa (x)
53. The Sacred Well of Chichen-Itza (x)
54. Climb Ayers Rock, Australia (x)
55. Follow River Jordan from Sea of Galilee to Dead Sea

Swim in:

56. Lake Victoria (x)
57. Lake Superior (x)
58. Lake Tanganyika (x)
59. Lake Titicaca (x)
60. Lake Nicaragua (x)

Other:

61. Carry out careers in: Medicine and Exploration (studied pre-med, treated illnesses among primitive tribes) (x)
62. Visit every country in the world (30 to go)
63. Study Navaho and Hopi Indians (x)
64. Learn to fly a plane (x)
65. Ride horse in Rose Parade (x)
66. Igauca Falls, Brazil (x)
67. Victoria Falls, Rhodesia (x) (chased by a warthog in the process)
68. Sutherland Falls, New Zealand (x)
69. Yosemite Falls (x)
70. Niagara Falls (x)
71. Retrace travels of Marco Polo and Alexander the Great (x)
72. Become an Eagle Scout (x)
73. Dive in a submarine (x)
74. Land and take off from aircraft carrier (x)
75. Fly in Blimp & balloon & glider (Glider only, so far)
76. Ride elephant & camel & ostrich and bronco (x)
77. Skin dive to 40 feet and hold breath 2.5 min. underwater (x)
78. Catch ten lb. lobster and ten foot abalone (x)
79. Play flute and violin (x)
80. Type 50 words per minute (x)
81. Make a parachute jump (x)
82. Learn water and snow skiing (x)
83. Go on a church mission (x)
84. Follow John Muir trail
85. Study native medicines and bring back useful one (x)
86. Bag camera trophies of elephant, lion, cheetah, cape buffalo, whale (x)
87. Learn to fence (x)
88. Learn Jujitsu (x)
89. Teach a college course (x)
90. Explore depths of the sea (x)
91. Watch a cremation ceremony in Bali (x)
92. Appear in a Tarzan movie (he now considers this an irrelevant boyhood dream)
93. Own a horse, chimpanzee, cheetah, ocelot and coyote (yet to own a chimp or cheetah)
94. Become a ham radio operator (x)

95. Build own telescope (x)
96. Write a book (on Nile trip) (x)
97. High-jump five feet (x)
98. Publish an article in the National Geographic (x)
99. Broad-jump fifteen feet (x)
100. Run one mile in 5 minutes (x)
101. Weigh 175 pounds. (still does) (x)
102. Perform 200 sit-ups and 20 pull-ups (x)
103. Learn French Spanish and Arabic (x)
104. Study dragon lizards on Komodo Island (boat broke down within twenty miles of island)
105. Visit birthplace of Grandparents in Denmark (x)
106. Visit birthplace of Grandparents in England
107. Ship aboard a freighter as a seaman (x)
108. Read the entire Encyclopedia Britannica (has read extensive parts of each volume)
109. Read the Bible from cover to cover (x)
110. Read the works of Shakespeare, Plato, Aristotle, Dickens, Thoreau, Rousseau, Hemingway, Twain, Burroughs, Talmage, Tolstoy, Longfellow, Keats, Poe, Bacon, Whittier and Emerson (not *every* work of each)
111. Become familiar with the compositions of Bach, Beethoven, Debussy, Mendelssohn, Lalo, Mihaud, Ravel, Rimski-Korsokov, Respighi, Rachmaninoff, Paginini, Stravinsky, Tchaikovsky, and Verdi (x)
112. Become proficient in the use of a plane, motorcycle, football, basketball, bow and arrow, lariat, and boomerang (x)
113. Compose music
114. Play Clair de Lune on the piano (x)
115. Watch fire-walking (in Bali and Sunam) (x)
116. Milk a poisonous snake (x) (bitten by a diamondback during a photo session)
117. Light a match with a .22 rifle (x)
118. Visit a movie studio (x)
119. Climb Cheops' Pyramid (x)
120. Become a member of the Explorers Club and Adventurer's Club (x)
121. Learn to play polo (x)
122. Travel through the Grand Canyon on foot and by boat (x)
123. Circumnavigate the globe (x) (did it four times)
124. Visit the moon (someday, God willing)
125. Marry and have children (x) (had 5 children)
126. Live to see the 21st Century (will accomplish at age 75)

Whether you're sixteen or sixty, you are still a person of many dreams. Now, write down all your wishes, dreams and aspirations, no matter how misty they may be. Be audacious when it comes to making your dream list Keep in mind the concept of regrets, keep in mind those dreams which are floating about in the mists of your mind. After you've written down some of your dreams, some of your wild ideas, then come back and clarify what your goals are in vital areas.

1. _____

2. _____

3. _____

4. _____

5. _____

6. _____

7. _____

8. _____

9. _____

10. _____

11. _____

12. _____

13. _____

14. _____

15. _____

16. _____

17. _____

18. _____

19. _____

20. _____

Which wish are you going to fulfill first? _____

_____

_____

When? _____

_____

_____

It's Up to You

Three scamps who lived in a small town were always trying to pull one over on the local sage, the wise man of the community. No matter how hard they tried, they could never outwit him, never outsmart him.

One day, they caught a baby robin. They thought, this time we'll fool him for sure. They formulated a plan. They decided to approach the old man and hold the bird behind their backs, and say to the old man, "This bird in our hands, is it dead or alive?" And if he said it was alive, they'd squeeze the life out of it, and if he said it was dead, they'd release it, and let it scamper away.

And so they went to the old man, and put their plan into effect. They said to the old man, "This bird in our hands, is it dead or alive?"

The sage, seeing their plan, looking at them with his piercing, steel gray eyes said, "That choice is up to you."

And so it is with you. You hold in your hands today a dream, many dreams perhaps. Will those dreams be given life? Will they take wing? Or will they fall dead? That choice is up to you.

> *If one advances confidently in the direction of his dreams, and endeavors to live a life which he has imagined, he will meet with a success unexpected in common hours.*
> —Thoreau

Chapter 4

Gaining Confidence

"We tap our potential by gaining confidence from our achievements..."

Give yourself credit for all that you have achieved; accept yourself as a fantastic achiever. Achievements provide us with great personal insight. When we acknowledge the changes we've encountered and successfully overcome on the road to our achievements we can see that those problems became our great advantages. Not only have you turned your problems into *advantages*, in solving your problems, you were exercising self-direction and self-determination. Through the process you expanded your circle of influence. More important, you were gaining an introduction to yourself, to your greatness, your potential.

These experiences helped introduce you to yourself in terms of your specific strengths, your inherent, unique capabilities. Those strengths and characteristics understood, combined and properly applied will allow you to overcome any and all future obstacles. They give you the courage to set higher goals, make stronger commitments, offset your natural weaknesses, and, in fact, turbo-charge your performance.

You have had many experiences when you have turned disadvantages into advantages. If you had been writing the script of your life, you would *not* have included this scene, and yet you turned that event into an advantage. You made something positive out of it. You turned your lemon into a lemonade. You turned your scars into stars. You turned your adversity into an advantage. I know this is true for you. I'm also aware that most of us are not as skillful as we could be at noticing, cataloging, analyzing and celebrating these successful experiences.

Even after we've turned adversity into advantage, we place too much energy on the wrong question: the "why me?" question. Instead of rushing on to the next chapter in your life after overcoming adversity, see what can be learned from the experience. Develop the ability to see the advantage that can be gained from an "after-action report."

After you have developed the discipline to do an after-action report, stop and say, "Gee, that's great. You know, that disadvantage really did turn out to be an advantage. I'm glad this happened to me. I'm glad this went differently than I'd wanted it to." This is a wonderful, positive attitude, a very helpful attitude, certainly more constructive than stumbling through life complaining about what's happened or getting stuck in the retelling of the story.

> *One machine can do the work of fifty ordinary men. No machine can do the work of one extraordinary man.*
> —Elbert Hubbard

Reflect on Success

By developing the ability to recognize your strengths, those specific strengths which caused you to succeed, you will be able to fully benefit from all of your past and future experiences.

These strengths include creativity, courage, confidence, enthusiasm, integrity, the ability to analyze, decisiveness, initiative, determination, persistence, calmness, centeredness, awareness, insightfulness, determination, communication, perspiration, clarity, humor, optimism, and so forth.

Most of us are better trained in the art of discovering weakness, foibles, short-comings, and foul-ups than we are in discovering strengths that we can lead from, fall back on, and leverage from. Developing the habit of analyzing your successes rather than rushing past them and spending excessive amounts of time in bemoaning your failures is the foundation of developing true wisdom. It is the starting point toward turbo-charging your performance.

In exploring your past successes, look at the fabric of your life and, in that fabric, woven through your life, will be revealed your successes and the strengths that contributed to them.

Take note of at least six of your past successes. After you've written down enough about your successes for you to get the *feeling*, the true *feeling* of your *success*, take the next step and write down the positive qualities and traits these successes reveal in you.

For example, one student, after the completion of this exercise, wrote:

Past Success: *Gained confidence and endurance after joining an aerobics class, even though I was intimidated by being only one of two men out of thirty women, and no other klutzes in the class, plus a history of back trouble.*

Strengths Applied: *Determination, patience, drive, persistence.*

New Strength Derived: *Ready to set new physical goal and challenges.*

Key each of your successes by entering one of the following symbols:

"P" for Physical Success   "$" for Financial Success
"F" for Family Success   "S" for Social Success
"C" for Career Success   "*" for Spiritual Success

Date	Key	Describe the Success	Describe the Feeling

What qualities or characteristics did it take for you to accomplish each of your past achievements? Think of things you have completed—the books you have read, courses you have taken, apprenticeship training programs, roles in a play, the position you always wanted, your athletic achievements, academic successes, and so forth.

We have not been trained to think in terms of qualities, and certainly not in terms of positive qualities. We think in terms of events and actions. We think in terms of effects, not causes. There are no random, spontaneous events. We live in an orderly universe—a world of cause and effect. Your qualities are the causes of all the effects in your life.

To get you started, here are more than a hundred positive qualities and traits. Pick the ones that you think most contributed to your past achievements. Think about your life—your unique gifts, talents and experiences. We learn by knowing and trusting rather than by doubting and fearing.

Look at all the learning opportunities life has given you. Now determine to learn, really learn, from those experiences. Discover truths and insights about the world and people around you, yes, but more significant is what these lessons have taught you about yourself, and your ability to reach deeper and higher.

Positive Qualities and Traits

Accommodating	Adaptable
Admirable	Adventuresome
Agreeable	Ambitious
Attractive	Aware
Awesome	Big-hearted
Brave	Bright
Calm	Careful
Caring	Cautious
Cheerful	Colorful
Communicative	Competent
Composed	Confident
Congenial	Considerate
Contented	Convincing
Courageous	Creative
Decisive	Delightful
Determined	Devout

More Positive Qualities and Traits

Direct	Discreet
Down-to-Earth	Dynamic
Eager	Easy-going
Effective	Empathetic
Encouraging	Energetic
Enjoyable	Entertaining
Enthusiastic	Exciting
Expressive	Faithful
Fearless	Firm
Fluent	Friendly
Generous	Gifted
Good mixer	Good listener
Good-natured	Happy
High-spirited	Honest
Humble	Humorous
Impressive	Ingenuity
Initiative	Insightful
Inspiring	InterestingIntuitive
Kind	Leader
Loving	Masterful
Motivating	Obedient
Open-minded	Outgoing
Persuasive	Pleasant
Poised	Precise
Productive	Proud
Organized	Quick
Quick-thinker	Quick-witted
Receptive	Refined
Reflective	Resourceful
Seeks high-quality	Sensitive
Smart	Sociable
Soft-hearted	Soothing
Spontaneous	Stimulating
Strength of character	Strong
Superior	Talented
Tenacious	Thoughtful
Tolerant	Unassuming
Unruffled	Unselfish
Vigorous	

Now list your qualities, those traits that have enabled you to succeed, that have enabled you to accomplish all that you have accomplished.

I am:_____

_____

_____

_____

_____

_____

_____

Be Confident

I was in my office late last night when the phone rang. "Is this Turbo; is this Larry Dennis?"

I said, "Yes."

The young man on the line said, "My name is Scott, and I listen to your motivational message every day. I work for a tux shop company with fifteen locations here in the Northwest. I'm just hourly, but we get a lot of complaints, and we need to improve our customer service. I told the General Manager in Seattle about you, and he asked me to give you a call."

Scott was empowered. I could hear him flex his muscles of self-esteem and confidence. By contrast, the Plant Manager in Seattle gave me eight documentable reasons why his local plant doesn't have the power, autonomy and ability to make the changes needed to deliver superior world-class customer service. The Plant Manager's facts were sound, but the disempowerment that comes from concentrating on the limitations came across loud and clear. Facts are never as important as attitudes.

For the sake of excellence, stand up and speak out like Scott did. You'll flex your muscle of self-esteem, you'll radiate confidence, and you'll be turbo-charged.

Chapter 5

Taking Charge

"...accepting responsibility for our present..."

This is another fine mess I have gotten me into.

—Pogo

Marty told our Leadership Lab, "I was buying a used car through a local dealership where I knew the general manager. The salesman asked me to sign all the forms and paperwork involved with the purchase. I didn't bother to read what I had signed until later, and it was then that I learned I had purchased about $300 of life and disability insurance that I did not want or need. The lesson I learned is to always read the fine print."

It won't help you to blame, shame, scream, or steam. It won't make any difference. What makes a difference is to learn your lesson and go forward with your life.

What is Responsibility?

In its simplest form responsibility means the ability to respond.

In a larger sense, responsibility implies an obligation; to consider oneself answerable for; accountability.

What do we want in our children? Responsibility.

Clyde, a district manager for a major mass merchandiser, was cleaning up his garage after finishing up some framing projects. He looked over his shoulder and saw his 13-year old stepson, Pip, sweeping the garage floor—*sweeping the floor!* Clyde hadn't even asked him to do the job. "What are you doing?" Clyde asked, shocked.

Pip's response was, "I'm sweeping the floor," and then Pip said, "because I want to be responsible."

What do we want in our employees? In our co-workers? Responsibility.

One of the greatest compliments anyone can give you is to say, "You are responsible." Which is to say, "You can be counted on!"

Can others count on you? Do you keep your promise, or do you make excuses? Do you step in when needed? Do you make the extra effort required? Do you have to be supervised, or do you *take the initiative*? Do you think things through, anticipate what will be needed, question and find solutions?

No Excuses

How can you enhance your ability to respond; how can you improve your responsibility? How would you describe your level of responsibility? The ability to respond, to accept full moment-by-moment responsibility for your present is the single most empowering thing you can do. This eliminates the victim role from your journey.

Through your creativity, your use of imagination, your visualization, your decision-making style, your people skills, your communication methods, your attitudes and enthusiasm, or your lack of these qualities, you have gotten yourself where you are. The qualities and talents you possess can help you develop the ability you need to move onward and upward with your life.

Tell yourself the microscopic truth, especially about those things that go wrong. Telling the microscopic truth, especially to yourself, is your jump-start to true personal empowerment. "If I can get me here, I can get me out of here."

Accepting responsibility gets you out of the victim mode, gets you on top of things and enables you to move on with power. Anytime you allow yourself the luxury of making excuses you move into a powerless position.

Don't pity yourself because you have a weakness. Don't look for excuses that flatter your vanity. Leave the crowded valleys of mediocrity. Climb to the heights. In areas of responsibilities, instead of endeavoring to excuse yourself, analyze each so-called experience of failure. Ask the question, "what part did I play in this?" even when it seems that you played no part in it; even when it seems it was entirely someone else's fault and responsibility. Be as analytical as a scientist in a laboratory. Be impeccably honest with yourself.

In your analysis, always begin by looking at what *did* work.

Turbo-charged people are not outer-directed, other-directed or outer-stimulated. Turbo-charged people are self-directed and self-stimulated.

Scott told us a wonderful story about his early years in college. He had a law professor (a crusty older gentleman) with very strict student office hours. Scott told us that when he went to see his posted grade after a mid-term, he couldn't believe his eyes. He'd scored 59, the third lowest grade in the class. He went over to the drinking fountain, splashed some cold water on his face, walked back to look again—still number three from the bottom. He couldn't believe it because he knew the material cold.

Scott went directly to the professor's office, knocked on his door. The professor said, "Can't you read? I'm not in." Scott said, "Sir, I know I have mastered the material. I may have misunderstood, I may have put the bar in the wrong place, but I want to take the test over again." The professor re-scored the test. Scott had a 94. He was number three from the top in his class, not from the bottom.

Scott told us that the lesson he learned is the importance of standing up, speaking out, and being counted, putting your convictions to the test.

Be Responsible. Put yourself on the line, put your convictions to the test. If you believe it, act on it. The benefit you'll gain is self-actualization, full achievement, strong self-esteem—the kind of self-esteem that can only come when we act on our beliefs.

Ask For Help

Bob, the shipping manager for a large bakery, told our Leadership Lab, "When I first started working at the bakery in 1980 I was a truck loader. Part of the job was backing the trucks up to the loading door. They asked me if I could drive a truck, and I said, "yes," which was the truth, because I could drive a truck—forward. They didn't ask me if I could *back-up* a tractor trailer rig.

"The first night I was on the job we had six trucks to load, and one tractor trailer to unpack at the front of the loading door. As I gingerly backed the first truck up to the door my heart was beating, my pulse was racing, and I was glad to discover that the truck bumper matched perfectly to the rubber bumper on the dock. I backed up carefully until I bumped into the dock bumper—no problem!

"After loading all six trucks it was time now to unpack the longer, larger tractor trailer truck. I needed to back it up to the loading dock. My confidence had been growing throughout the night. When the truck got back to the dock I heard a loud, sickening sound of wood crunching. Quickly, I pulled forward thinking, 'I must have missed the rubber bumper.' I jumped out of the cab of the tractor and did quick time to the back of the truck. What I discovered was that the longer trucks were also higher off the ground, and I was backing the truck right *through* the loading dock door! Wow, was I embarrassed when I had to go to my supervisor and tell him what I had done.

"The important lesson I learned is: if I don't know how to do something, anything, admit it and ask for help! I learned at a deep emotional level that it is easier and safer and more productive to ask for help than to let my ego, my pride, my fear block me from asking for the help and for the training I need to perform with precision and excellence."

Be perfectly honest about your ability to perform. Never be afraid to tell the whole truth about your experience, background, training and capabilities. Ask for help. Ask for coaching. Be the kind of leader who is known for your openness. Be coachable. The coachable person says. "Thanks for the input; thanks for the idea; thanks for your concern." The coachable leader doesn't defend or give excuses. Instead, the coachable leader asks for help, guidance, input and suggestions. Ask for help! Ask for training!

The benefits you will gain are successes that will build one upon another. Your confidence will grow. Your career won't go back and forth, and you won't crash. Instead, doors of opportunity will open smoothly for you. You will be successful by leveraging off the knowledge and know-how of all the other members of your team.

Be Open to Criticism

Remember Pearl Harbor? It's been fifty years since that infamous attack caught us so unprepared. But there's a great wealth of knowledge that tells us we could have been prepared if we had just listened. There were messages intercepted and sent, warnings sounded—we now hold this as common knowledge. Why didn't we listen and prepare ourselves for the horrendous attack? Our arrogance and pride, our stubborn disbelief that anyone would really try to attack us, prevented us from being prepared.

The personal lesson we can learn from this experience is the importance of being open to feedback, to criticism, to the unexpected. We must fight off the tendency to insulate and isolate ourselves from the truth; we must prepare ourselves for the changes that are taking place in our own world, to ready ourselves for the inevitable.

Preparing for tomorrow today is an important part of your plan for accepting full responsibility and will build your enthusiasm and self-confidence. You will be ready to be turbo-charged.

There is another side to being open to criticism.

When the last hostage, Terry Anderson, was set free after almost seven years in Beirut, we heard a story of courage, determination, and faith, a story that honors the character of a man and his supporters. Why were he and the other hostages released? Because their captors found no value or advantage in continuing to hold them.

No one can intimidate you, cause you to cower, imprison you, intimidate you with threats and demands if you refuse to be intimidated. If you know your principles and stand firm on your standards, you will intimidate the intimidator.

Becoming fully responsible for your attitudes under any and all circumstances by standing firmly on your convictions and drawing on your inner strength is a major part of your personal program to be turbo-charged.

Recharge Your Batteries

Brian told our Leadership Lab, "About two weeks ago I became aware of a number of people who were absent from work because of being ill. In the back of my head I can remember thinking to myself, 'Boy, it would be nice to be sick for a couple of days, just kick back and read; take it easy.' I'd been working extra hard at the time, and I was also stepping out of my comfort zone on a regular basis, all of which takes extra energy. I was tired and wanted a break, so I visualized becoming sick to get the break I needed.

"Last Tuesday I noticed a funny feeling in my throat. A kind of sensation that I had learned in the past meant a cold was coming on. By the end of the day the funny feeling had turned into a violent cough. Each time I coughed, it felt like someone was pulling fish hooks out of my lungs. From then on my health went into a nose-dive. My feet felt like they were frozen in blocks of ice, while my head was sandwiched in a waffle iron set on high. My back felt like it had been beaten with a rubber hose. My eyeballs felt like they were being forced out of their sockets, while each tooth in my skull felt like it was impacted.

"I went to the doctor and begged him to shoot me. I felt so bad I wanted to die. He dryly stated that I had the classic symptoms of the flu and to go home and rest for a couple of days. He also said that I would probably not be back to normal for at least four to six weeks.

"What I learned from this experience was that I need to take the time to recharge. My job and learning new skills takes a lot of energy. I need to recognize this and schedule time to recharge my batteries."

Be aware of the energy needed to accomplish new goals. Allow yourself time to get away from it for awhile so you can come back to all of it in a new light. The benefit you will gain will be an increased resistance to falling ill.

When I have a cold I'm reminded of a sign I saw in an office that said, "No Sniffling." It's hard to describe the graphic impact of the sign, but it had tears running down off the letters; no, it was like a nose running down in each one of the letters of the word "sniffling." I thought to myself, "How disempowering it is to sniffle; how often I sniffle and find myself sniffling—complaining about this and complaining about that." And what I realized is that whenever I find myself in a sniffling mode, I rob myself of my power, and I rob others of power, too. I don't attract winners (and I need winners around me all the time), and I lose my ability to perform at high levels.

A part of accepting full responsibility is avoiding the inclination to sniffle about anything (the weather, the hole in your socks, your boss, your prospects, the lack of support you have from those around you). Resist the temptation to sniffle. If it bothers you enough that something needs to be done about it, take some specific action that would help solve the problem, but don't sniffle. Sniffling never looks good on you. When you stop sniffling, when you resign from sniffling, when you make it your practice never to sniffle, others will notice you; you'll stand out, others will be lifted by your courage and confidence; and you will be turbo-charged.

Be Calm

A contractor who provides specialized services to our firm had received my letter offering him 33% less than he'd asked for doing a certain job—an important job. Because of the specialized nature of the work he provides for us, it would be *very* difficult for us to find anyone else with his qualifications. He'd called to say that he had to insist on the full amount he'd asked for. We discussed other aspects of the job and my desire to work with him, both in the short and long term. I didn't try to push him, beg or persuade him. I didn't try any fancy footwork.

When I arrived back at my office late in the afternoon, there was a note from him with approved dates and a reduced price—a price that we can both live with.

What I learned from this experience is to be responsible for what I give my energy to. I'm sure that an angry, put-out, pushy response to his seeming rigidity would have gotten me a mirrored response.

Accept the responsibility for remaining centered when you feel pushed. Be careful about giving up your power by lashing back, trying to prove you're right. By remaining calm, collected, centered, you retain your energy, and often you'll earn the same flexible response from others.

I arrived at 6:30 and began to rearrange the room in preparation for a Leadership Insights Breakfast for Associated General Contractors (AGC). The breakfast was advertised to start at 6:59 a.m., but there was no coffee, no food. I inquired, and finally, at 7:39, the food arrived. By this time, I was well into my program, one we had spent weeks planning and advertising. Much of our Fall plans depend on the success of this promotion. To put it mildly, I wasn't pleased. When I showed the Catering Manager our contract, she produced another contract. Who's to blame? Well, the truth is, the restaurant was late, and our Office Manager didn't document all of our requests clearly.

The larger truth is that I didn't do everything that was my part in this little drama. Don't blame and shame: it's always disempowering. Blaming others removes our responsibility (our ability to respond), disempowers us, makes us feel out of control, and can put us into the victim role.

Look at everything that isn't working or could work better for you. Ask yourself, "What can I do to improve the process?" You'll find personal empowerment in accepting responsibility and in taking action.

When I conducted a meeting for the management team of a telephone answering service, the receptionist greeted me with an enthusiastic welcome, asked if I'd like coffee, and returned a moment later saying, "I'm sorry, we're temporarily out of coffee." I said, "No problem. I'm really a tea drinker."

I was directed to the conference room. A few moments later, the receptionist arrived with a thermos of brewed tea. When I realized what she had done (it took a moment for it to sink in), I said, "Wow! Really? I can't hardly believe it."

She said, "This is your lucky day; you'd better buy a lottery ticket."

I said, "I agree, you've made me feel very fortunate, but you'll have to go a little further to convince me to buy a lottery ticket. If you do, it will be my first."

I don't believe in that kind of luck. Henry Ford said, "The harder I work the luckier I get." And I know that persistent, intelligent effort has its rewards. I believe in serendipity, fortuitous occurrences that happen in our lives as we're actively engaged in the pursuit of our goal. A belief in "lottery luck" could rob us of our motivation. I prefer to believe in an orderly universe where cause and effect gets sprinkled with serendipity to motivates us to jump into the flow of life, apply ourselves toward our goals and keep our eyes open for the joyous unexpected.

Turn Disadvantage to Advantage

Mike is the president of a capital equipment manufacturer. His logging-related business is suffering, really suffering. Is this good news or bad news? Shakespeare said, "Thinking makes it so." Who's thinking? Mike's thinking. The concept of accepting responsibility for our present is something we get to do fresh and new every day.

In tough times, you either wait or create. Wait for the economy to turn around, or create new markets for old products or new products for old markets.

Mike and his team have invented, literally invented, a new process, a new way of applying laser technology to his log-cutting equipment—equipment which at one time used hard cutting blades only. Mike's patent is pending. He's optimistic, excited, confident that this new invention will posture his firm in such a way that his competition will only see his tail lights.

Sometimes it doesn't require a major change to create incredible new value. All the Wright brothers did, in the final analysis, was put flaps on the ends of the wings. This enabled them to fly. The point is, you may be experiencing a challenge in your life or business. Is this good or bad? Thinking makes it so. So be responsible to look for the good in everything you experience, in everything you encounter, determine that your thinking will be such that you'll invent new ways of doing what needs to be done. You'll find new markets for old products. You'll find new services to provide your markets. You will be turbo-charged.

I listened to thirty leaders share their experience in meeting a challenge head-on, overcoming the challenge and going on to win bigger than ever. David, a glass installation contractor told us about his experience in 1985. After working hard to build his business for two years, they won the largest contract their firm had ever received. They took the specifications to their extrusion supplier to begin production. No go. The supplier said they couldn't deliver.

Where do you go now? What do you do now? Quit? Blame? Feel sorry for yourself? Sue somebody?

David and his partners drew together, took the situation to their customers, and began manufacturing the extrusions themselves. Now, six years later, they've been highlighted in national architectural magazines featuring the Portland Convention Center, a major part of their work. What had been the darkest days in David's career turned out to be the best thing that ever happened to his business.

Look for the good in the difficulties that come your way, find a way to turn every disadvantage into an advantage. Be responsible. The next time you're faced with a challenge, large or small, sit back and say, "Great!" Ask, "Where's the gift in this situation?" And go into action. This determination to find the good and build on it will help you grow, will help you benefit from every experience, and you will rise to new heights.

We went to Salem to meet my brother, Bruce, and his family for our annual trip to the Oregon State Fair. We didn't pick the best night weather-wise—it was clear when we left Portland, but by the time we arrived at the State Fair, at about 7:00, there was a steady drizzle.

We went into the amphitheater, put down newspapers on the metal seats, and waited for the show. We covered ourselves with our umbrella and black plastic. Finally, at about 8:00, the Oakridge Boys began to sing. They sang "Elvira," "My Baby's American Made," and all their familiar songs. The umbrellas came down, and everyone began to clap. The amphitheater was packed. No one in the theater seemed to let the rain dampen their spirits. And in spite of the heavy gusts of rain that blew in on the Oakridge Boys, they sang along like troopers. Everyone seemed to gain even greater joy out of the event as a result of the rain.

How is the change in weather affecting your spirits? Someone may say something critical toward you or your work, put you down, rain on your parade, criticize your ideas, or fail to recognize the contribution you make. It's not what others say to you that really matters; it's what you say to you after they've said it. Our response is determined by us, and us alone. Nothing that anyone says to us can affect us; it's only what we say to us after they've said it that matters.

Be responsible for your own attitude. Enjoy the party, make it fun, and you'll be turbo-charged.

Shoulda, Coulda, Woulda

Have you ever felt under the circumstances? Visualize someone who is under the circumstances. Does he or she look burdened down, slumped over, emitting heavy sighs like someone carrying the weight of the world on their shoulders? Contrast this with someone who is on top of "things," on top of "it," or "with it." This is the opposite of being under the circumstances. People under the circumstances have no power, their lives depend on the economy, the boss, the spouse, the circumstance.

Emerson said, "I have discovered the people who get on in this world get out and make their own circumstances." How can you get on top of things, be the powerful person you are capable of being? You can actually *talk* yourself into weakness or power. Words have the power to strengthen or debilitate you. Here are some power robbing words:

TRY
HAVE TO
SHOULD
BUT

"I could've been a contender," the failure says, looking for sympathy. "I would've amounted to something if I hadn't dropped out of school," mourns the drifter. "I should've bought AT&T back in '56," sighs the guy asking you to lend him ten bucks. "If only I'd married the other guy," complains the welfare recipient.

Choose your words carefully, for words have power. Emerson said, "Words are living things, you cut them and they bleed—you put them down and they wiggle around." And it's true, words have power, whether we direct them at others, or at ourselves.

"Should," as Star Trek's Spock might say, "What an interesting concept, but one that's completely irrelevant." But what "should" you have done? Well, first of all, you can't "should." What a waste of time to say, "I shoulda." When we do this we are parenting, shaking our fingers at, and talking down to ourselves or others. And how do you react to this treatment? You cower (no power) or you become defensive (no power). "Should" endeavors to fix blame in

the past tense. Do you want someone to blame, a "whipping boy," or do you want to learn from the experience and move one? Fix your gaze on the future, the past is past. Sometimes you can pacify yourself by saying, "I should have." You can excuse yourself, you can get off the hook, but you're not fooling anyone but yourself, and you're not accepting responsibility, learning from your action (or inaction), empowering yourself and moving on to new accomplishments.

"*Have to*" is another enslaving phrase. If you find yourself saying, "I have to...," you are putting yourself under the circumstances, disempowering yourself. Look at the empowerment that comes from saying, "I get to," or "I want to," or "I am." When you use these phrases, *you choose*, no one makes you. The difference between a word and a right word is the difference between lightning and a lightning bug. Now there's a contrast in power!

We never do the things we "try" to do. We do the things we do. Can you hear the whine in "try," the hopelessness, the powerlessness? Trying implies that you're not able, you're not in control. Why not assert yourself? "You shall declare a thing and it shall be established onto you." That's right, put yourself at risk; make a promise; make a commitment; discover what power issues forth when you say, "*I will.*"

A class member heard this concept, caught this power in a recent class. She said, " I have tried to quit smoking so many times. This time I *will* quit," and she did. Five people in that class quit smoking. Notice the power of an idea and notice how, when we start to improve in one area of life, it spills over to all other areas.

One of my favorite lines from George Lucas' great movie, *Return of the Jedi*, takes place in a scene between Yoda and Luke Skywalker. Luke is feeling sorry for himself, feeling overworked, feeling helpless, disempowered, and at the end of his rope. He says, "Why should I try so hard to become a Jedi Warrior when I am stuck here on this Godforsaken planet?" Yoda says, "What do you mean stuck here?" Luke says, "Look at my spaceship, as it sinks further into the muck and mire." Yoda says, "If you can pick up a rock with your mind, you can pick up a spaceship." Luke with a great degree of doubt says, "I'll try." Yoda says, "No, not try; do or not do." And so it is that you will only do the things you decide in advance to do. Why say "try," when you could say "will"? Because you're afraid? Rise above the fear of failure, the fear of being at risk. Notice how your power and confidence grows as you begin to put yourself at risk by saying, "*I will.*"

"*But*" is a weak word, a word that accompanies excuses, "should have" and "would have." With "but," excuses flow. Notice the power you have when you cut your buts and excuses, when you use a nice, crisp period instead. Another negative use of the word "but" taints approval or praise. If you say, "He's a good salesman ..." and follow it with a "but," you would have been better off if you had withheld the praise in the first place. Again, use a nice, clean period.

Take responsibility to train your mind to look for the good—to find and see the good in all situations, people and events.

Turn your back on all the good or bad that's past and live in the present moment. Refer to the past to gain the turbo-thrust, to plan for the future but do not drag the past into your present, or worry about the future.

Take responsibility by forgiving everyone without exception, including yourself.

Take responsibility for decisions. Notice the power your praise and approval has when you impact others with a compliment. And notice the extraordinary sense of power and empowerment you have when you accept full responsibility—no blaming or shaming.

When you create the kind of environment that creates harmony in your life, and provides an atmosphere you enjoy, you are taking responsibility for your inner peace. When you choose the kind of food and drink that benefits your body, you are taking full responsibility for your own good health. Is that book nourishing your mind and heart? And does that TV program really improve the quality of your life?

When you are willing to take responsibility for your decisions, you will experience a surge of energy and power. The quality of your life, and your success in your career, will improve in direct proportion to the decisions you thoughtfully and considerately make today.

Taking full responsibility for your attitudes, words, and feelings can be your most important step toward living the turbo-charged life.

Now, rewrite the following sentence using as few words as possible :

> "I guess I should've checked to make sure that copies were made, although had I been told how important it was, I would've taken better care to remember where I put the original, but under the circumstances lots of things could've been done better."

If you used more than four words, do it again.

Chapter 6

Commitment

"...and committing to our goals."

The secret of success is to decide what you want out of life and go about gathering together the means and materials by which to achieve that end.

—Aristotle

We are by nature goal-striving creatures. We pursue our goals whether or not we've articulated them, whether or not we believe in them. We are, by our very nature, creative creatures and we are co-creating. We create our own world. The world we create is a garden of Eden, an inferno, or something in between. And what we create is determined solely by the quality of our thoughts.

As a salesman was driving across Montana's big sky country, he saw an old, abandoned billboard on the side of which was a bulls' eye, and right in the middle of the bulls' eye there was an arrow. As he drove a little further he saw an old barn. On the side of the barn there was an old Bull Durham sign, and in the middle of that sign there was a bulls' eye and right in the middle of the bulls' eye was an arrow.

He took the next exit, and as he was coming in to the little town he saw an abandoned service station on the side of which was a bulls' eye, and right in the middle, an arrow. Then he saw an old general merchandise store and on the side was a bulls' eye, and in the middle, an arrow. By this time his curiosity was thoroughly piqued. He stopped into the local pub to wet his whistle and asked the bartender, "What's this with all these bulls' eyes with arrows right in the middle?"

The bartender said, "Well, the fellow who does it is sitting right over there." The salesman looked over, and there at a table in the darkened corner of the bar a fellow was slouched over an empty glass. "That guy?" he asked.

"Yep, the bartender said, "he's the one. If you buy him a drink he'll show you how he does it."

So the salesman said, "Give me the drink," and he walked over, sat down at the table and said, "How in the world do you get all these arrows right in the middle of those bulls' eyes?"

The guy chugged his drink down and said, "Well, let me show you." He pulled an arrow out of his quiver, put it in his bow, pulled it back, and sent it zinging across the room and into the wall on the far side of the bar. Then he picked up a little bucket of paint, walked over and drew a bulls' eye around the arrow.

And that's how too many people set goals. Whatever they hit is what they call their goal. Obviously, goal setting is far more than circling what you have hit. Goal setting is deciding what you want to hit and then taking all the ability, skill and knowledge you have and focusing in that direction.

Setting Goals

In July of 1962, I went to work for the Crescent Tool Company of Jamestown, New York, as a missionary salesperson. I called at retail hardware stores and lumberyards throughout the Midwest. The initial stages of my training consisted of two weeks at the Jamestown headquarters. I toured the factory, visited with he various ous departments heads, learned about the policies and procedures, how to fill out orders and expense records, read some articles on selling, went to lunch with the Vice-president of Sales, and began to get a clear picture of my role, goals and responsibilities. I arrived at the goal of selling $3,600 worth of tool displays a week, or $720 per day and $14,400 a month.

My marketing efforts were made up of three primary activities: participating in wholesale hardware shows, staffing booths and writing future orders with show-special prices, calling directly on Ace, Cotter, HWI, other retail stores who were members of wholesale jobbers and co-ops, and traveling with the wholesale sales representatives of the traditional wholesale jobbers. I traveled with a different salesperson every day. On those days when there was no salesperson to travel with, I made independent calls on hardware stores and lumberyards throughout my territory. In six months I worked in thirteen states.

I often left my home in Anderson, Indiana, on Sunday afternoon so I could be at a store when it opened Monday morning at 8:00, and then I worked until Friday or until I achieved my goal of $3,600 worth of tools sold for the week. I resolved that if I had not sold $3,600 worth of tools, then I would work until 9:00 Friday nights. I suppose I would have worked on Saturdays if hardware stores would have been willing to see me on Saturdays. It wasn't easy during the weeks I was behind on my goals, and still hundreds of miles from home, to continue calling on hardware stores, but I can tell you that I did.

After a few months, the company tool display van I was driving broke down. I had to take it back to Jamestown to pick up a new truck which was being custom outfitted for me. I arrived two days before the new truck was completely outfitted. Meanwhile, the treasurer of the corporation met for lunch. He told me, "Larry, you've sold more tools over the past six months than anyone we've ever had in your position, and that includes the Vice-president of Sales, who started in the same position twenty years ago."

The experience proved to me that if I set a high goal and commit to it to the extent that I permit nothing else to stand between me and its achievement, I can do outstanding things.

> *I worry that our lives are like soap operas. We can go for months and not tune into them, then six months later we look in and the same stuff is still going on.*
>
> —Jane Wagner, *The Search for Signs of Intelligent Life in the Universe*

Planning for Success

Clarity of purpose is, without question, the secret of success—no matter how you define success. Webster defines success as: *"The progressive realization of some worthwhile goal."*

Without a goal there is no success. With a goal, even if we've taken only the smallest progressive step toward that goal, we are, by Webster's definition, a success. At the dawning of Western civilization, Aristotle captured the essence of successful living. He pointed out that we must determine where we are going and what our purpose is before we set out. Repeated surveys, decade after decade, have shown that fewer than 10% of us have clearly defined goals. Even a smaller percentage have their goals in writing, as few as 2%. A smaller percentage still review their goals on a daily basis, as few as .5%.

Aristotle's suggestion—that we decide what we want from life and then gather together the means and materials, the tools by which to achieve that end—makes complete sense. Psychologist and author Denis Waitley notes, "All winners set goals. Corporations and institutions have clearly defined plans, but only top achievers in life seem to have adopted the same kind of game plan in their own personal lives."

As we interview young college students who are to "gather together the tools and materials" by which to achieve success, we find that many of them don't know what they want to do after graduation. I recently asked a young lady who is a senior in a college of journalism what she wanted to do when she graduates. Her answer was, "I'm not sure; there are a lot of options available to me." This is not reported in a spirit of criticism; it's a frequent observation. We often put the cart before the horse "doing, acting, working, learning" without being sure why or where we are going.

All riches and all material things that anyone acquires through self effort begins in the form of a clear, concise mental picture of the thing one seeks. People who know exactly what they want in life and are determined to get it, do not stop with wishing. They intensify their wishes into a burning desire and back that desire with continuous effort based on a sound plan.

Success...it is focusing the full power of all you are on what you have a burning desire to achieve.
—Wilfred A. Peterson

You want to be a success, or you wouldn't be reading this book. The odds are against you, but the universe is for you. You were created to succeed; you are a goal-striving mechanism. It all begins by deciding. The most important question you can ask is, "What do I want?" *Clarity* and *singleness of purpose* will remove you from the masses and place you in the classes.

Success is the progressive realization of worthwhile goals, to be measured more by difficulties overcome than by targets hit. Success is an inside job and it looks different for each of us. It includes successful, harmonious relationships, financial prosperity, physical well-being, spiritual connectedness, and a strong sense that you make a positive difference in your world.

How will you know when *you* are successful? You can confirm your success by checking your list of goals.

We must see that we don't run out of goals and wants, so that we always have something new and exciting to plan and work for. We need that "carrot on a stick." If you plan to be less than you are capable of being, you'll be unhappy all of your life.

A want that is satisfied is no longer a want. To be healthy and fully alive you need new goals and wants. Goals fill our lives with excitement. Remember your first car? Your first home or apartment? How full of excitement and anticipation you were! But after you have achieved these things, the car is three years old, the house is ten years old, the excitement fades and these things seem everyday. So sit down and make a new want list!
                                                    —Earl Nightingale

Live all you can. It's a mistake not to. It doesn't so much matter what you do, as long as you've had your life. If you haven't had that, what have you had? What one loses, one loses; make no mistake about that. The right time is any time that one is still lucky to have. Live!

The right time is now! Don't think that the future will somehow be better. Learn to live all you can, now. It is worth giving thought to how you can make your life more interesting and vivid. Older people are always saying to younger people, "You don't realize how lucky you are." I suppose that means that they didn't either!

Henry James

Write it Down

I met with Kevin Saturday morning to help him prepare for the first session of the Leadership Lab. As we talked I asked him about his goals. He reached in his billfold, took out a 3X5 card folded into three parts, on which he'd written, "Job a year from now." He talked about his specific salary goal, and on and on, in very specific detail. Is there any question in your mind from what little I've told you so far about this sales rep., that he will reach his goals? I can't be certain that he'll reach the exact goals he's written on his 3X5 card, the thing I am absolutely, totally, 100% certain of, is that he's going to reach more of his potential, and achieve more with his life than 90% of us do. The reason: He's taken the step of writing out his goals. They're specific, they're measurable, they're tangible, and he carries them with him wherever he goes.

While I was living in Cleveland, Ohio, and working for The W. Bingham Co., I saw a small ad in the newspaper by the S.M.E. (Sales and Marketing Executives Club) for an inspirational Sales Rally. I purchased a ticket for $7.00, a good deal of money for me at that time. I went to the auditorium in downtown Cleveland, walked in, and took a seat near the back. You need to know that I was raised in a town of 30,000 to appreciate how intimidated I felt being in the major city of Cleveland and walking into a large hall with thousands of professional salesmen. I remember very little of what the speaker said now, but I do recall him saying something like, "You can do whatever you dream you can do, you can become more than you dreamed you're capable of being..." Somehow he stirred a spark inside of me that night and I began to dream. That's all it was at the time. I began to dream of being in front of an audience just as he was, and making an impacting, inspiring presentation.

A problem in my own goal setting, and a problem I share with thousands of people I've coached over the last quarter of a century, is impatience and the resulting lack of persistent, concentrated effort. Twenty years, almost to the day after I walked into that auditorium in Cleveland, Ohio, scared and intimidated, I stood on a platform along with Bob Richards, the decathlon champion and Olympic gold medal winner. We were at the Red Lion Inn in Portland, Oregon, before 3,000 salesmen on behalf of the Portland SME. I attempted to inspire and motivate the audience just as I had been inspired and motivated twenty years earlier. Later that night I heard Bob Richards say, "You get what you go for!"

Far more important than my experience, or that of any Olympic medal winner is *your* experience in setting and achieving goals. You've heard and read the stories, and you know that no champion in any field of endeavor has ever succeeded by coincidence. Far more important than their natural ability is their ability to set a goal and commit themselves to that goal. Through that *commitment* they are able to achieve their greatness. What's more important than my story or theirs, is *your* story, your experience. Do you "get what you go for"?

While I was the Ordering Officer at Ft. Storey, Virginia, I became good friends with the president and owner of Roanoke Auto Parts, Red Huntley. Red loaned me the recording, *The Strangest Secret*, by Earl Nightingale. Earl Nightingale's classic inspired me again and again as I listened to it over and over in my Army barracks room. I can still hear his melodious voice say: *"Whatever you plant in your mind, be it deadly nightshade or life-giving corn, the mind is fertile and willingly reproduces whatever you plant in it."*

That is the secret, the greatest secret, the strangest secret in the world. The Roman Emperor Marcus Aurelius said, *"Your life is what your thoughts make it."* Echoing that concept centuries later, William James, a Harvard University psychologist, wrote, *"The greatest discovery of my generation is that men can alter their lives by altering their attitudes of mind."*

I once had the privilege of hearing Earl Nightingale in person. I sat in the front row of the Ford Auditorium, downtown Detroit. I'd been listening to him on the radio, read his other materials, and ultimately listened to his tape series, *Lead the Field*. I heard these words, which made more sense to me than anything else I've ever read or heard on goal setting: *"If you will examine in the lab of your life those goals that you've wanted consistently for the last five years, so long as you haven't wanted something just as badly which was inconsistent with your goal, you have achieved that goal, something better, or are well on your way to achieving it."*

As I examine my life I discover it is true. Those things I had wanted for five years, which were not inconsistent or incompatible with other goals which I said I wanted just as badly, I had either achieved or am well on my way to achieving. Examine your own life to see if that is true for you. Check it out. Haven't you achieved the goals that you have consistently pursued, goals that weren't conflicting with other goals you gave equal importance? Goal setting is the essence of a self-directed life.

Over the past quarter of a century my class members have said, "I don't know what I want." There is an inclination to speak in vague, general terms when trying to describe what we want. Most people are better at describing what they don't want than they are at describing what they do want. For example, I've had hundreds of salespeople tell me in personal interviews, "I don't want to be rich." Socrates counseled his students centuries ago to "Know Thyself." So, before you read any further, answer this question: "What do I want?"

I Want:_____

_____

_____

_____

Singleness of purpose is the great secret to successful living. If you can't describe what you want in specific, measurable, tangible terms *you don't know* what you want.

During his *Adventures in Attitudes* seminars, motivator Bob Conklin tells participants, "All great achievers have been great planners. They have the ability to organize their activities, sort out the unimportant things and invest their time in productive, meaningful effort. Research has revealed that people who set goals are happier, earn more money and have more successful job records than those with no goals."

From your dream list that you wrote out in Chapter Five, you can begin to develop some specific goals. A goal, as we define the term, is specific, measurable, tangible, in writing, and has a timeline. Putting a timeline on your goals adds the element of accountability. Many class members have told me, "I know what I want, I don't need to write it down." If you know what you want, why would you resist writing it down? Writing clarifies thinking.

Why do you think some people have trouble writing out their goals? When I've asked class members, they've always quickly responded, "If I write them out, then there's accountability." And that's absolutely true. That's the very reason why it's very important for you *to* write them out, to put your specific goals in writing.

Often the same people who say, "I don't have to write out my goals, I know what I want," are the very same people who forget what they went to the grocery store for, forget their own anniversary, or the birthday of a friend or relative. Imagine operating a business without an appointment book! We're talking about an appointment with your future. Your goals *must* be in writing.

A Goal Planning Outline

In order that your self-image can be improved and your life's potential can be achieved, it is necessary for you to set goals for each compartment of your life. By categorizing goals, you are not attempting to separate them, but, rather, to connect them in a harmonious, supporting network, so that all goals become inter-related, each a part of the others, and work together. This is the "whole person" concept.

Here are some areas you may want to concentrate on:

Career: This includes all the desires or dreams of your chosen pursuit, your life's work. Consider establishing levels of accomplishment, advancing your career position, or developing more effective skills.

Financial: Your financial goals might involve getting a raise, getting out of debt and building a specific net worth by a certain date.

Family: You could include improving family communication, organizing family time, or improving relationships with your spouse, parents, brothers and/or sisters.

Spiritual: These goals might include developing a prayer consciousness, tithing effectively, or learning how to incorporate spiritual practices into daily living.

Physical: Goals such as eating more selectively, losing or gaining weight, improving physical appearance by means of a new wardrobe, learning how to use make up, starting an exercise program, or giving up smoking.

Mental: Would include such goals as enhancing capacity for learning and remembering (including names), eliminating certain erroneous mental attitudes, or taking additional classes that could be used for advancement.

Personal Relationships: Goals such as developing a better relationship with your spouse (or getting a divorce), establishing a relationship with a member of the opposite sex, acquiring new friends, or releasing old relationships.

Feelings: You might include goals which reflect positive attitudes such as experiencing joy each day, regardless of the circumstances, or surrendering blame, resentments, irritability, and guilt.

Your goals will fall into three general categories: *do, be* and *have.* The "do" and "have" goals are the easiest to define. The "be" goals are far more difficult. When we've thought in terms of goals in the past we've generally not thought in terms of "be." The truth is, before we can *have* anything we don't now have, we must *do* something we're not now doing. Before we will consistently do things differently than we're doing them now, we must *be* different in some important ways than we now are. Here are some samples of the kinds of do, have and be goals you might be interested in, in the vital areas of your life.

1. *"Things I Want To Do"*: Take a cruise or expedition, write a book, return to school, climb a mountain.

2. *"Things I Want To Have"*: A dream house, a new car, a doctorate, my own darkroom, a ski boat, new wardrobe, beach house.

3. *"Things I Want To Be"*: Your total concept of the person you want to be—patient, tolerant, well-read, open, caring.

Action is living. My "Do" Goals include: _____

_____

_____

_____

_____

Targets make the game of life more fun. My "Have" Goals

include: _____

_____

_____

_____

_____

I can only have what I'm willing to be. My "Be" Goals include: _

_____

_____

_____

_____

_____

In order for your full potential to be reached, set goals in each area of your life. By connecting your goals in a harmonious, supporting network, they become inner-related and work together synergistically. Instead of creating the fragmentation of unclear or conflicting goals, take this opportunity to write out your goals in each of these areas of your life and the *first three major steps* you need to take in order to achieve them:

My Career Goals: _____

Step 1 _____

Step 2 _____

Step 3 _____

My Financial Goals: _____

Step 1 _____

Step 2 _____

Step 3 _____

My Family Goals: _____

Step 1 _____

Step 2 _____

Step 3 _____

My Spiritual Goals: _____

Step 1 _____

Step 2 _____

Step 3 _____

My Physical Goals: _____

Step 1 _____

Step 2 _____

Step 3 _____

My Mental Goals: _____

Step 1 _____

Step 2 _____

Step 3 _____

My Personal Relationship Goals: _____

Step 1 _____

Step 2 _____

Step 3 _____

My Emotional Goals: _____

Step 1_____

Step 2_____

Step 3_____

    Writing out your goals will help you crystallize your thinking. There is a fear connected with goal setting: the fear of failure, the fear of missing the mark. In other words, the related accountability that goes along with goal setting. There is an eraser on your pencil. If you want to make new commitments, you can always change your mind. I urge you to be careful about changing your mind too easily. There is a difference between changing your mind and giving up. Thoughtful living will help you know the difference. When you find that your values have changed, that your world has sufficiently altered, that you are no longer committed to your original goal, don't be stubborn. Admit it, and determine what your new goals are.

    Goals must be positive, not what you don't want, rather what you do want. You can't visualize what you don't want; you can visualize what you do want. Goals must say "how much, how many and by when."

    Deadlines are the foundation of commitment. Deadlines are the adrenaline boosters. Deadlines are the instigators of achievement, and inventiveness. A goal without a deadline is merely a philosophical statement.

    After you've compiled your list, ask yourself these questions about each goal:

Is this goal bigger than I am? _____

Will it stretch me to a size I can't now fit? _____

Is this something I want?_____

Is it really important to me? _____

Will it bring good to myself and to others?_____

Will it make the world better in some way? _____

Do I have a burning desire for its achievement?_____

What is the deadline for achieving it?_____

Get others to talk about your goals with you. Find someone to believe in them with you. Delay, procrastination, comfort can cause you to lose sight of your vision.

Determine Priorities

Using the lists you have made of the things you desire and want, your "do, have, and be" list, assign a priority to each one. Number them according to their importance to you. Assigning priorities helps you decide which goals are of major importance and deserve your immediate attention and which ones could wait until some future time.

As you look at these goals, you will recognize the fact that some of them represent major undertakings that may require ten, twenty or thirty years to complete. Goals of this kind, long range goals, represent your ideals, your ultimate goals, a purpose for your entire life. It is extremely important to begin work immediately on the most important goals of this kind. You will quickly recognize other goals that might be classified as intermediate goals or short range goals because of the relatively shorter time required to achieve them. The most important of these goals also deserve immediate attention.

Many of your short-range and intermediate goals actually constitute steps toward the fulfillment of your most important long-range goals. Suppose, for example, your long-range goal is to be president of the company where you are now employed although your present position is several levels away from that position. One of your short-range goals might be the completion of an important project that would qualify you for a promotion. An intermediate goal might be to become a vice-president of the company. Achievement of both the short-range and intermediate goals would move you closer to ultimate fulfillment of your long-range goal.

People frequently fail to achieve their long-range goals because they consider these aspirations to be so far in the future that no action can be taken today. Intermediate and short-range goals keep you on the path to your ultimate long-range goal because they constitute the activities applicable to today and the actions you can take this week that will move you closer to your ultimate goal.

List, in order of their priority, the three most important long-range goals for your life. These goals might take several years or even longer to achieve. Next, list your five most important intermediate goals in the order of their importance. These might be goals which you could achieve in one to three years or perhaps even in five years. Finally, list some short-range goals, those you can achieve this year, this month, or even this week. You might wish to list as many as ten of these important short-range goals in the various areas of life.

When you have identified your most important goals, you will know where to start planning. Remember that the goal-setting process is a continuing way of life. Periodically, you will plan new short-term and intermediate goals to advance farther along the road to achievement of your long-range goals. As time passes, you may find it necessary to adjust, add to, or delete some goals as you grow and change. When priorities change because of changed circumstances or changed personal desires, it is appropriate to change your written goals. Because these goals represent your personal desires, any adjustment or change is a matter of your own personal choice. Change is evidence of growth. Never be afraid to change your priorities of adjust your ultimate goals.

Make sure these goals are high enough to be meaningful, worthy of your attention, interest and commitment, yet small enough that they are, when you stretch your mind, believable.

My top priority long-range goals are:

1. _____
2. _____
3. _____

My top priority intermediate goals are:

1. _____
2. _____
3. _____
4. _____
5. _____

My top priority short-range goals are:

1. _____

2. _____

3. _____

4. _____

5. _____

6. _____

7. _____

8. _____

9. _____

Establish Your Goals

Develop a written plan with dates for reaching your goals. Pick an important "to-do" goal that is measurable and meaningful and answer these questions:

1. What is your "to-do" goal? _____

_____

_____

2. Why is it important to you? _____

_____

_____

3. When do you want to achieve that goal? _____

_____

4. What roadblocks will you need to overcome? _____

_____

_____

5. Who can help you? _____

_____

_____

6. What other resources or information do you need? _____

_____

_____

7. What can you do first to get started?_____

_____

_____

8. Who will you share your goal with, so they can cheer you on? __

_____

_____

9. How will you check on your progress?_____

_____

_____

Be specific, measurable and tangible in your goal-setting. Are you committed to your goals? If your answer is yes, and you stay focused, draw on your strengths as revealed through your past achievements list. You will reach your goals, and much, much more.

My plans for reaching my goals include: _____

_____

_____

Skill areas needed for me to reach my goals are: _____

_____

_____

If you set a goal, you've got the ingredients for success. You'll be on the path toward greatness. It will be like walking through two lines of people who are hitting you on the shoulder and hitting you on the back at the same time. They'll keep pushing you forward.

Go to Work!

When despair's sharp edge is near.
Go to work.
When your mind is racked with fear.
Go to work.
When your brooding o'er the past.
And the sky seems overcast.
Go to work.
When you haven't even a friend.
Go to work.
When you can't see light ahead.
And your utmost hope has fled.
Don't lie moping in your bed.
Go To Work!

—author unknown

Part Two

Fourteen Strategies
for Goal Achievement

Chapter 7

Excellence Today

(Strategy #1)

Steve, our Senior Associate, and I met to go over the second draft of a proposal we started writing a couple of weeks earlier. It was very difficult for us to decipher some of our notes. At the time we were writing our original proposal, the ideas were flowing so fast and we were both writing rapidly too rapidly, as it turned out, for us to be able to read our notes a couple of weeks later. Well, we finally worked it out, and we were able to put together most of the pieces, but it was frustrating, a waste of time. It could have been done a lot more efficiently.

The lesson I learned is the importance of doing it right the first time, and, if I have to correct things, correct them while they're still warm in my mind.

Accept responsibility for doing it right the first time. Xerox estimates that up to 85% of their administrative time is spent doing things over. By doing things right the first time, you'll save time, be a more important team member, lower your frustration level, improve your performance. And this improved performance will help turbo-charge you.

> *The best preparation for tomorrow is to do today's work superbly well.* —Sir William Osler

There is within mankind the urge to be different, better, to change and improve. This is mankind at best. This urge to be more than I am, better than I seem to be, comes from the *perfect* center of us. This urge to count, to make a difference, is not something to take lightly. There is a purpose to this quiet urge to make the best of ourselves.

But why do some people live below this level? They seem to be rather complacent about the idea of being better than before, of making a positive difference. They seem bent on destruction.

The first ingredient of meaningful goal achievement is the element of commitment. It's important to remember that someone is always watching. That someone who's always watching is you.

A number of years ago I attended a workshop conducted by Dick Morgal, my regional manager from the home office of the company I was associated with at the time. As we were walking from Stouffer's North Land Inn, in Southfield, Michigan, to Stouffer's restaurant, a block or two away, Dick turned to me and said, "Larry, your long-range success is guaranteed."

"Why do you say that, Dick?" I asked.

He said, "Because you understand the secret to long-term goals achievement."

I was a little taken aback, and my response was an honest one. I said, "What *is* the secret to long-term goal achievement that you say I understand?"

I wish I could imprint Dick's response indelibly on your mind, on the forefront of your brain. I believe deeply in the truth of what he said, and what he said was, "The secret to long-term goal achievement is commitment to excellence in what you are doing today."

Yes, it's just that simple. The secret to achieving that one-year, that five-year, that ten-year, and that twenty-year goal *is commitment to excellence to what you're doing today!*

The inclination to worry about tomorrow, do long-term planning, and to wait until we're in a better position, or a better time to commit ourselves to outstanding excellence is the inclination of the average person. So, the person who rises above mediocrity is the person who commits himself to excellence, every minute of every day of his or her life.

Desire Success

Do you remember the story of the young man who called his girlfriend and said, "I love you so much I'd climb the highest mountain, I'd swim the broadest sea, I'd walk on hot coals and cut glass."?

Following this flowery display of emotion, his girlfriend sighed, "Are you coming over tonight?"

He said, "I'll be over if it doesn't rain."

Commitment is "have to." Look it up in Webster's. To commit oneself, it says, is to "speak or act in such a manner as to bind oneself to a certain line of conduct." Notice the word "bind." It doesn't say anything like "subject to the following conditions." That's not commitment; that's equivocation.

Commit yourself to stretching goals. Tell others, and enlist their support. The benefit you will gain is the inspiration and support needed to achieve the impossible.

Mike, our printer, stopped by our office to drop off the new versions of our Leadership Lab Manuals. Mike opened his Minuteman Press about sixty days ago. The manuals looked great. As we proudly looked through them, Mike said, "I spent the night last night at my shop—that's twice this week. He said, "At 2:00 a.m., I was so rummy that I rolled out my cot and spent the rest of the night there." He went on to say, "It was worth it though, because this is the first day since we opened our business that I really felt on top of things."

Mike's paying the price, and his business is showing it. Over 90% of the businesses that start in America fail before their fifth year of operation. Mike's business will prosper. I know this for many reasons. Mike's a great planner: he investigated dozens of franchises before he bought this franchise. Mike's a great salesman: he has a strong track record over a decade of successful selling experience. And Mike is personally willing to pay the price, do whatever it takes. He's totally committed. And there's a guarantee that you too will enjoy long-term success. Plan, develop your presentation abilities, make unreserved commitments, and you too will experience long-term success.

To buy the business Mike took out a second mortgage, and then moved his family out of the house to the guest house over the garage so he could rent out the main house to make payments on the second mortgage. Now, that is real commitment, and it is paying off.

> *Struggle always comes before success. For most artists, when they have arrived at what the public and critics term success...all the pain and struggle—all the strife and anxiety that preceded—is forgotten.*
>
> —Jascha Heifetz

Excellence Tomorrow

Build your desire to fulfill your long-term goals. This desire must be stronger than your natural inclination toward immediate gratification. Statisticians say that 70-90% of us will never reach the goal of maintaining our ideal body weight unless we can forego the natural inclination to fulfill our appetite's desire for immediate gratification.

I heard the story long ago of a young boy who went to the village sage, the man who was known to be the wisest of all men. The young boy had looked around his town and realized that most people lived, as Thoreau said, *"Lives of quiet desperation."* They lived from one day to the next, concerned only about their indebtedness, their bills. They were not fulfilled in mind, body or spirit. Their relationships lacked gratifying fulfillment of their desires. And so, being a thoughtful young man, he said to the sage, "Tell me the secret to success."

The sage, being a very wise man, said, "I can't tell you the secret of success, but I will help you discover the secret, if you do exactly as I ask you to do."

"I will," the boy said.

Seeing his sincerity, the sage said, "You must trust me, and do what I ask you to do."

The young boy said, "I'll do anything. I want to know the secret of success. I don't want to live as those around here live, beaten-down, barely getting by, living humdrum lives."

"Come with me, then," the sage said, and walked down to the banks of the nearby river. There, he took the boy by the hand, and began to walk out towards the middle of the stream. Soon the water was up to the boy's waist, then up to his chest, above his shoulders, and now above his mouth, and finally, above his head.

The old man was taller than the boy, and soon the boy began to struggle in the old man's grasp, trying to raise himself above the water. The old man, instead of helping him up, pushed his head down, held him down. Then, at the precise, right moment, the old man removed his hand, and helped the boy up. The boy's mouth came up above the water and took a mighty, sucking gasp of air. Fighting back his tears, he said, "What are you doing to me!?"

The old man asked, "Just now, what did you want more than anything in the world?"

The boy said, "Air!" And it was true that at the moment he did want a breath of air more than he wanted anything in the world.

The old man said, "When you want success as badly as you wanted that breath of air, success will be yours."

You must want success more than immediate gratification. Your body will never be as healthy as it could be if you seek the immediate gratification of plopping down in front of a television set. And your relationships will not be what they could be if you seek the immediate gratification that comes from watching sitcoms and soap operas instead of risking intimacy with your potential friends.

You must be willing to do whatever it takes to achieve your goals. This commitment goes beyond reasonableness. After you've written out your goals, maturity requires that you acknowledge the fact that in the past you may have set similar goals, if not the same goals, and failed to achieve them. That does not mean that this goal cannot be achieved. It simply means you must do something differently in order to achieve the goal. One definition of insanity is "doing the same thing in the same way and expecting a different result." What is your plan for generating total commitment to your goal?

Chapter 8

Imagineering

(Strategy #2)

No great genius ever existed without some touch of madness."
—Seneca

When Larry Becker and I were both about twelve years old and talking about cars, I said, "I'd never want a Cadillac." He said, "I wouldn't either." And we began to justify all the reasons why we wouldn't want a Cadillac. Well, the truth of the matter is we couldn't dimly imagine ourselves having a Cadillac and therefore we wouldn't open ourselves to the possibility. It just seemed chic and cool for us to talk about why we didn't want one. What we were doing was disassociating from the stretching goals.

Develop an image of who you want to be. Picture in your mind the able, earnest, useful person you desire to be, and the thought you hold will hourly transform you into that turbo-charged person.

A Persian prince was born a cripple, a hunchback. On his twelfth birthday, his father asked him what he wanted, saying to the youth standing before the court, "Son, I will give you anything you want for your birthday. You can have half my kingdom. Your wish is my command."

The boy said, "Father, I want a statue of myself."

His father, broken-hearted, said, "Oh, son, please."

The young prince said, "Father, I want a statue not as I stand before you today, crippled, bent over, a hunchback, but straight, tall and erect."

And so his father had a beautiful marble statue carved of his son, straight, tall and erect. He had the statue placed in the garden in the center of the courtyard. Each day the young prince would stand before the statue, staring up at this characterization of himself, straight, erect and tall. Each day he stood there, gazing up, straining, his head bent back. Slowly, imperceptibly, steadily, he began to change, until, on his twenty-first birthday, when his father called him into the royal court to ask him what he wished for his birthday, promising him anything in the kingdom, anything in his power, the prince stood before his father straight and tall.

We become the images we hold in our minds. The most important thing is to create an image, an image of ourselves—the dynamic, confident, successful person we desire to be—and to hold that picture steadily in our minds. Each day, stand before that perfect picture and look at that image until one day we shall stand in the middle of our fully-realized dream.

This practice will fan the flame of sincere desire to realize the wishes of your heart.

Visualize

Visualize picking up a lemon that has been in the refrigerator. Feel it, experience it with all your senses. It is cold. The skin is waxy, but not entirely smooth. Feel the texture of the lemon. It's firm, yet yields a bit when you lightly squeeze it.

Now, pick up a knife and slice that lemon in half. The skin resists slightly, giving off a tart, fragrant, fruity smell. Now raise the lemon halfway to your face. Smell the two distinct odors of the rind and the pulp, one milder than the other. Now, squeeze some juice of the pulp into your mouth. The sharp, acidic taste produces sudden saliva in your mouth to help dilute the lemon juice.

Did you smell the lemon? Did you salivate? That's your imagination at work. If you have imagination, you can visualize.

Use your powers of imagination, of visualization to set up positive expectations for yourself, self-fulfilling prophecies, in every aspect of your life. You *can* if you *believe* you can.

In his best selling and extremely important book, *Psycho-Cybernetics*, Dr. Maxwell Maltz, a plastic surgeon, described his experiences in performing plastic surgery. In changing the outer image of the patient, Dr. Maltz discovered that, as his patients saw themselves differently their behavior changed dramatically, and in many instances their life experience became dramatically altered. Patients who refused to see themselves differently continued to experience the same kind of life as before.

Whatever we vividly imagine, ardently desire, sincerely believe, and enthusiastically act upon, must inevitably come to pass! Walter Knott

Self Image

Our self-image determines the level of our performance. It can be a governor that holds us back. As you implement the strategies in this section, your self-image will improve and you'll be turbo-charged.

I am not talking here about adding to your brain power, your I.Q., although we now have evidence that the brain literally grows in size and capability with regular exercise. Nor am I talking about changing your basic physical stature, although your body can be immeasurably enhanced through right eating, exercising and rest. I am talking about you as you are, and about changing the way you see yourself.

1. You have a self image. This image was formed before you were seven years old.

2. You will not persist in actions that are inconsistent with the image you hold of yourself.

3. Your self image can be changed, adjusted, "improved" through the practice of the right principles.

Let's examine these three statements. The first says that everyone has a self image, and that this image is formed early in life—by the age of seven. It may even have started forming while you were in the womb. We are very responsive to suggestion during the early discovery months, the first 36 months. Most of us continue to be responsive until we're twelve, sixteen or eighteen, becoming less responsive as we mature.

In the early years, input from authority figures is taken quite literally. You are "slow, stupid, sick, weak, pale, unorganized, sloppy, clumsy, uncoordinated, a sleepy-head, selfish, mean, stubborn, backward, lacks energy, ugly," etc., or you are "bright, beautiful, full of life, enthusiastic, loving, kind, open, neat, organized, healthy, alert, quick to learn," etc.

The younger you are, the more responsive you are to programming, and the less able you are to qualify the input, whether negative or positive, whether constructive or destructive, helpful or hurtful. As you grow older, you tend to conform to this pre-determined self view *trying never* to perform in a way that is inconsistent. This, of course, sets up a reinforcing pattern, because your self view after the age of accountability is determined *not* by your experiences but by your perceptions of your experiences. So, as you sprint along the track of life, if you "set a world's record" and your self-image is that of a loser in that particular area, you will say, "I was just lucky this time. I bet their stop watch isn't working right." If your self view is that of a winner, you will say, "That is just like me. I am always getting better. I am a trail blazer, a record setter."

These responses are reinforcing, causing the experience to repeat or deplete. *You will not persist in actions that are inconsistent with the image you hold of yourself.*

However, your self image can be changed if you practice the right principles. The science of behaviorism is based on the theory that basic behavior "tends" to repeat itself, and that past behavior traits will predict with almost absolute certainty future performance. Most major companies rely on various behavioral tests to help in selection decisions. The widespread use of tests designed to predict future behavior based on past behavior is strong evidence of the soundness of the statement that we always conform to our self-image.

So, how can you change your self-image? Through the use of visualization, empowering self-talk, image books and the other strategies described in the second half of this book, you will have the tools needed to change your self-image, to turbo-charge yourself.

A man's life is dyed the color of his imagination.
—Marcus Aurelius

An Image Book

Being comes before having, first within, then without. An Image Book is a powerful tool to reconstruct your mental belief system about yourself and the way you see and experience your world. The right brain (feeling, feminine, subjective) responds to images and feelings and cannot tell the difference between an imagined experience and one that is real. Our creative, subjective mind cannot reject as being untrue, wrong, or invalid the images and feelings presented to it. By its very nature, our mind must, in time, reproduce as outer reality all that it believes and accepts in the secret workshop of the brain.

Your Image Book is a tool that, when properly used, will help bring into focus the new forms, shapes, colors, patterns, textures, and things you select and project upon the mental screen of your creative imagination.

Your Image Book is a tool for re-engineering your self. Its pages consist of pictures, words and symbols that represent your higher self. When you see yourself as successful, confident, and free of fear, you will be able to bring about the most astonishing changes in yourself. By focusing the energies of your mind upon the qualities you desire to express, the things you wish to have, and the events you wish to experience, your creative imagination will cause them to manifest. Your Image Book pages can help overcome any character defects and shortcomings by reflecting desired strengths and aspirations.

> *Getting your imagination captured is almost the whole of life. The minute the eyes of your heart are enlightened, the minute your imagination gives you the picture of your path, your goal, your aim—it is as good as done. The way to become the architect of your fate, the captain of your soul, is to have your imagination captured*   —Rufus M. Jones

Your Image Book is *the way* to capture your imagination. Your outer world and all that it contains is but the visible expression of your inner state, all you have pictured as being real or true for you.

If you want to change your life experience, then change your mind, change the way you think and feel.

Your self-image determines your life experience. Your experiences on a moment-to-moment basis can be no higher or lower than the invisible image you have of yourself. Your self-image is comprised of your thoughts and feelings about yourself, whether these are conscious or subconscious, true or untrue.

Mind (thinking and feeling) = self-image
Self-image = You, the visible representation of the state of your mind

1. Cut out from magazines and newspapers words and pictures which are descriptive of the real you, your higher self. You may not believe them now, but they describe how you intend to feel about yourself. Reach so far beyond your present concepts about you and your world that these new ideas almost embarrass you. The pictures you choose should not include the face, so that you can more easily identify with the new image you are portraying.

2. Create one or more pages on the various aspects of your life you want to have changed, developed, or expanded. Let these pages describe your wonderful inner qualities, such as your femininity or masculinity, your emerging self-confidence, your warm and loving nature. Let these pages show you as an effective and caring spouse, parent, or friend. Let your developing spiritual nature have its way as it creates pages describing the new outer and visible part of your so that your own concept of life can undergo a dramatic transformation. This will be true for your surroundings, your physical appearance, clothing style, and everything that comprises your world.

3. If you have a problem area, such as a lack of order or lack of organization, create a page affirming new order in your life.

How to Use Your Image Book

Using your Image Book is easy and requires very little time, yet the effort you put into working with it will bring dramatic results.

1. Review your pages daily. Pick times that fit best in your schedule, either in the morning before your day begins or in the evening before you sleep, preferably both.

2. As you look at the pictures and read the words, *feel* that you are

this person "now" and that everything on this page has already come into your life. Feel that the page is an accomplished fact, even if it isn't so yet. Remember, your creative imagination cannot tell the difference between what is real and what you are imagining. To have the page become "you" and part of your life, it needs to be a present tense experience, not a future one. Feel it now.

3. Your pages act as affirmations, and as goals firmly set in the mind. Focusing your attention upon them daily will cause your mind to work for you. Whatever you conceive of and believe in, you will achieve. This is accomplished by joining your conceptions with feelings of excitement, gratitude, and a sense of already having accomplished the things you are rehearsing in your mind.

4. In a very short time, it will take only a glance at a page to conjure up these positive responses. Other pages, in which you have really stretched yourself, may take longer for full belief, but it will come!

5. Knowing that you are taking action to achieve your inner and outer goals makes your life very exciting and fulfilling. Use the pages regularly. Your book may not yet be finished, but continue to work with the pages you do have while compiling the remainder.

Examine your Image Book regularly and ask yourself:

• When I read my Image Book, do my pages come alive for me?

• Do I read my affirmations with a positive, expectant, happy feeling, believing that they will come to pass?

• Am I aware of my negative inner self-talk that tells me I will not succeed in achieving my desired changes and goals? I know that as I take charge of my thinking, I take charge of my life.

• Do I see these pages as the future reality of my life?

• Do my affirmations include dynamic, descriptive words to express my goals and feelings?

• As adverse situations present themselves, do I use my Image Book to maintain my positive, confident feelings?

• Could I define my areas of desired change more clearly or more specifically? Do my Image Book pages reflect my goals in life?

- Am I making progress? Is there any evidence that I am moving toward my goals? If not, what changes do I need to make?

- Am I setting aside time daily to work with my Image Book?

The stoical scheme of supplying our wants by lopping off our desires is like cutting off our feet when we want shoes.
　　　　　　　　　　　　　　　　　—Jonathan Swift

Visual Aids

Keep your goals in front of you. Visual reminders will influence your thoughts. The reason we put a sign on the refrigerator, a note on the mirror, is to trick our minds. If your goals aren't so big that you are challenged to believe them, they probably aren't big enough. Where, in addition to your image book, will you put visual reminders of your goals?

You will never do anything consistently that is inconsistent with your view of yourself. To experience the fullness of life you want and deserve, go to work today on your self-image, re-engineering, re-inventing yourself. Take a dream or an experience you want and visualize it. Describe it, describe yourself in it, how you want to feel, what it looks like, how it sounds, see it working out exactly the way it would most please you. Write it down. Cut it out. Paste it up. Become your image and you'll be turbo-charged.

Chapter 9

Self-Talk

(Strategy #3)

Our lives are what our thoughts make of them.
—Marcus Aurelius

I often ask my audiences, by a show of hands, how many talk to themselves? Most people are aware enough to know that they do talk to themselves and raise their hands accordingly. I then comment, "I guess the other ten or twenty percent of you are asking yourself right now, 'Do I talk to myself?' The point is that we all talk to ourselves, endlessly, day in and day out."

Most of these internal conversations are unrehearsed and spontaneous. Research has shown that seven out of the ten thoughts we think are negative; most of our self-talk is limiting; some is even demeaning. Often our inner dialogue rationalizes our lack of performance, negotiates for lower goals, lower standards, arguing for our limitations.

You can take charge of your self talk, however, whether it's inner dialogue, mindless chatter, or outer utterances, and you can keep your attention on your goals. You can become more aware of your mind chatter by using pep talks, planned and spontaneous positive affirmations.

SELF-TALK: *Are you an Architect or Demolitionist?*

...often the private discussions carried on in the mind get carried to the outside, too. When we are in conversation with someone, our tone and chosen words reflect our on-going "mind chatter," sometimes projecting an image of low self-esteem or confidence.

Personal "put-me-downs" defeat us, but we can use self-talk to be an architect not a demolitionist.

Positive self-talk is just that...POSITIVE! When you choose mind chatter that builds you up, your foundation becomes stronger and will resist the occasional negative demolitionist comments, those from yourself or others.

Work on your self-talk dialog by keeping a journal or list of the things you say most often to yourself for a week. Review this inventory of personal vocabulary and circle the words and phrases that you would NEVER say to someone else for fear of hurting them. Now, ask yourself why you talk to YOU that way and begin immediately to replace all negative mind chatter with positive words and phrases that make you feel good.

Get in the habit of giving yourself compliments that are real and sincere, just as you would give to others. Practice saying positive phrases out loud in the mirror for a few days until they naturally come to mind. Be aware of how you are feeling during this time of self-talk rewording. It is natural to feel a bit silly, just don't allow feeling silly to become negative self-talk. There is a big difference between saying to yourself, "I feel silly doing this," and, "This is stupid and I am stupid to continue doing this."

Use words that show conviction for yourself and your career. Each day tell yourself (and others); "I am a professional"; "I am good and deserve good things"; "I feel confident"; and, "I like myself." Begin each day by telling yourself, "This is MY day and nobody can take it away from me," and then continue using healthy, positive self-talk so YOU don't take YOUR day away. Continue to be the architect of yourself and not the demolitionist.

Carly Kutz Holliday
Oregon Speakers Association Newsletter

Listen to what you say about yourself, especially when you are tempted to speak in a limited way about yourself. Say, "Until Now, I couldn't remember names"; "Until Now, I couldn't keep a budget"; "I was afraid of cold calls until Now." Never say, "I think I am catching a cold," say, "Health and wellness are flowing through my body right now." If someone says you are catching a cold, say "I am getting better."

Empowering Yourself

You have set a terrific sales pace; your performance is nearly 20% ahead of the same period last year. The regional manager compliments you on your performance and informs you that your quota for the next quarter has just been increased by 25%.

Limiting self-talk is when you say out loud or to yourself: "That's impossible! I'm cranking at top speed already, and I got lucky on a few big orders in the first quarter. That's why I'm 20% ahead of quota right now. There's no way I can close the year with a 25% increase!"

Empowering self-talk is when you say: "That's going to be a challenge. A combination of circumstances has helped to make my 20% gain possible so far. You can continue relying on my total commitment for the second half of the year. I'll do my best to meet the new quota, and I don't believe that the 25% increase is unrealistic."

Which salesperson sounds like the person who has a shot at hitting the additional 25%?

What future do you want? Is it possible to reach into your past and literally remake it through the use of your imagination? The answer is "yes." And through that same creative imagination you can script your future; you can literally direct the future. This is work, and it may require an outside director, but what work is more important than determining that your life will be "as you like it."

So, today, take a moment to review your past, and rescript those parts you would like to see differently. Your imagination and your sub-conscious mind cannot tell the difference between an imagined event and a lived event. Look into the future and re-script your future. This is necessary if you want your future to be significantly different from your past. As you do this, you'll get a sense of encouragement, a sense of optimism, a sense of excitement, a sense of enthusiasm. And this confidence, enthusiasm, and optimism will turbo-charge you.

Think happy thoughts. Let the child in you out to play a little every day; don't let the cares of life keep you from joy or plunder your happiness. If you allow (or force) yourself to think happy thoughts, you can fly, rise above the cares of today. In so doing, you can recapture the innocence, optimism, and creative spontaneity of youth.

Take a second to check it out. Are you letting the cares of life hold you down, weigh you down, keep you stuck? You can remove the fetters by changing your mind, switching to a happy thought. Watch what happens. You'll float above the circumstances of the day. You will have a freshness and an empowering perspective. So, do it now—think a happy thought. Hold that thought long enough to give your life a lift.

> *Thinking can help you make the most of your experience. Thinking is an experimental form of action. Action can be very expensive. There is no charge for thinking.*
> —Dr. Zaleznik

Word Watch

"Aren't you excited about the President's announcement and empowerment of the new General Manager?" I asked a management team executive.

"That's not what the President said," he replied.

"It's not?" I said, "What did you hear the President say?"

The executive had interpreted the President's words in an entirely novel way; he had heard what he wanted to hear, what he was prepared to believe.

Just as your eyes can play tricks on you through optical illusions, mirages, and the hidden faces in the art of Bev Dolittle, your ears can play tricks on you, too. We hear what we're prepared to hear, what we're willing to hear and willing to believe.

Listen, really listen, to the weak non-committal words you may be using. Put in their place, strong words of commitment. You will be turbo-charged.

A young lady came into a shoe department in a Los Angeles store, and asked our youngest son Loren for a pair of gold shoes to go with her gold dress. Loren said, "No problem," and dashed to the back of the stock room to find some in her size. The store has a four-pair policy (show four pairs of shoes to each customer). He said to his manager, "I'm going to *sell* her three pairs." Loren dashed back out with four pairs of shoes to show her. She'd set aside some additional ones. He described the shoes' features and benefits enthusiastically. Before she left, she bought *four* pairs!

Loren's powerful affirmation ("I'm going to sell her three pairs.") demonstrates that you really can declare what you want in life and get it, inch by inch. Not everything you declare is going to come automatically, but nothing you've wanted and achieved of significance has ever come without your having first declared it.

What do you want? Why not declare that you want it? "Declare a thing and it will be established unto you." Why not decide, right now? State it. Put it into words, and then put forth the actions necessary, the enthusiastic action required, and you will experience the thrust of a turbo-charger.

Joe McGuire knew how to sell. When he was selling Remington Rand electric typewriters in markets dominated by IBM and others, Joe had convinced himself that the Remington Electric was the best typewriter on the market.

Whenever a prospect made a comment about his typewriter, he would assume they were praising it. He didn't pretend they were praising it, he believed they were praising it because he believed it to be the best typewriter on the market. He had brainwashed himself to believe that because he knew that every salesperson had to learn to sell himself first.

If a secretary would comment, "Gosh, that's a big typewriter," Joe would comment, "I knew you'd like that it's heavy-duty and big enough to handle all of your work."

When a prospect would ask how much it cost, Joe would answer, "That's the best part about it—only $635." Some prospects were surprised and would respond, "$635?!" At that time, a manual typewriter cost about half that. But Joe would answer, "I knew you'd be surprised. Most people would expect it to cost a good deal more than that." Joe believed that, and that's why his customers began to see it as a real bargain.

—*Joe Griffith, Speaker's Library of Business (Prentice Hall)*

Give Yourself a Pep Talk

You've accepted the challenge, the whole gang is waiting for you to jump off the diving board, but your knees are knocking so hard you can barely climb the ladder. Or, you promised your spouse you would go in and have that "conversation with the boss," and you're about to knock on your superior's door. What you do in these situations is take a deep breath, and give yourself a pep talk. When you deliberately, intentionally, and consciously talk yourself into doing something, you've given yourself a pep talk. This motivational strategy is especially useful in emergency situations, or when you get into situations where your ego is at risk. The doctor says you'll have to exercise more; a book or workshop makes it clear that some changes have to be made; the challenge can come from any number of sources, but in order to meet that challenge some conversation with the self is necessary. These talks we really hadn't thought of as conversations, or weren't previously aware of at the conscious level are conversations nevertheless. We have all given ourselves pep talks.

You're familiar with the use of pep talks on the athletic field. Football and basketball coaches use pep talks as part of their regular arsenal. Many games have been won in the second half or in the last quarter because the coach found the right words that called forth and created an extra level of performance from the team. These are grown men and women, dedicated to performing at the highest possible levels. It is obvious that the pep talk has an impact on their performances. If a pep talk results in a higher performance level for them, we can expect it to have the same positive effect on us. The only difference is we have no one to give us a pep talk—or do we?

No one is more interested in your success, your performance or your achievements than you are. You can give yourself a pep talk. You do it all the time. Have you ever talked yourself into doing something you really didn't want to do, like getting on an exercise program, quitting smoking, losing weight, getting up in the morning and going to work when you were out late the night before and weren't feeling 100%? Have you ever talked yourself into going into the boss' office to bring up an uncomfortable subject? Do you remember talking yourself into asking someone for a date, or doing something that involved physical risk, like getting up on water skis or skydiving?

We've all talked ourselves into doing something that we were afraid of or really didn't want to do because of inertia. How did we do it? We kept talking to ourselves. We said things like, "You can do it. You'll make out fine. It will be okay." The more mature we are, the more self-directed we are, the more often we talk ourselves into doing what we want and need to do versus taking the path of least resistance and following the crowd.

Just as we've talked ourselves *into* doing things in the past, it is also true that we have talked ourselves *out* of doing things. These are negative pep talks. They are often subtle and intentional pep talks where we deliberately and intentionally have a heart-to-heart talk with ourselves. For this talk to have its greatest impact, the pep talk must be aimed at something specific, and it must be animated.

There must be a purpose, a goal, for a pep talk to have an effect. When you say, "I'm going to have a great day today," the goal is to have a great day. When you say, "We're going to have a great staff meeting," the goal is to have a great staff meeting. You might say, "I'm going to do a great job on this buying trip," or "I'm going to do a great job on this sales interview," or "When I talk to my employees about their absenteeism, I'm going to be positive, forceful, friendly, and effective." In each of these cases, you have a deliberate goal in mind.

A pep talk is also said out loud and is designed to achieve results immediately or imminently. Statements of intent are frequently accompanied by aggressive animation. You could beat on your dashboard and say, "I'm going to make a great sales call." You might punch the air and shout, "This will be the greatest presentation I've ever made!" You could clap your hands and say, "It's the greatest sales interview I've ever conducted!" Managers, before going into an appraisal interview might say, "This will be the greatest appraisal interview I've ever conducted." Before going into a selection interview, they could say, "This will be the greatest selection interview I've ever conducted." Before going into a safety meeting you might say, "This will be the greatest safety meeting I've ever conducted." Before facilitating a problem-solving conference, say, "This will be the greatest problem-solving conference our team has ever had!"

You could be sitting at your desk before going in to see your boss, and you bang on the top of your desk with animation (not so much as to call unnecessary attention to yourself) before you go into the boss's office. The purpose of the animation is to get the blood running.

Water at 211 degrees has no value. It's too hot to drink; it's too cold to sterilize anything with it; it doesn't make good tea; it won't percolate coffee; and it doesn't have enough intensity to drive a locomotive. All that's needed is one more degree. Water at 212 degrees changes its molecular structure. It's state is altered to steam. With steam properly harnessed, you can literally move mountains.

The purpose of a pep talk is to give you that one more degree. It's to get you going. It's to get your blood running, your heart pumping, and more importantly, to wake yourself up, jar yourself loose, talk yourself into doing something that you have the capability of doing, but for whatever reason—probably fear—you've avoided doing. So often we sell ourselves short. With a pep talk, you're selling yourself long. You're selling yourself on yourself, and you're selling yourself on your ability to perform the tasks that lay ahead.

Begin enjoying the experience and power of a pep talk. You will notice that you perform at a higher level. You will achieve more, have greater impact, be less self conscious, be more to the point and overall have more impact as a result.

Chapter 10

Affirmations

(Strategy #4)

You are today where your thoughts have brought you. You'll be tomorrow where your thoughts take you. You can't escape the results of your thoughts, be they base or beautiful or a mixture of both, you'll gravitate toward that which you secretly most love.

—James Allen

Affirmations are verbal tools used to change attitudes, build confidence and restore faith. An affirmation consists of well-chosen words selected to convey a positive idea for the purpose of influencing your thoughts and feelings—and thereby your life. To affirm is to state positively that a thing or condition is so, even in the face of all contrary evidence. This truth, this power, is the substance of every good thing you can possibly desire if you know how to use it. All that you want, need, and desire is at this very moment trying to happen to you, but it cannot until you learn to say, "Yes!" to those things and conditions which have not yet occurred. Negative conditioning can be replaced by positive input.

You need affirmations—statements that affirm the attitudes or habits you wish to cultivate—to serve as reminders and to build your confidence that you can reach your goals. Affirmations that work are stated with great feeling. Affirmations are used to define ourselves based on a positive reflection of our experiences and successes rather than letting other people define us. It is essential that you stir up positive feelings. It's in the positive feelings that the healing, turbo-charging process will occur. You will be bringing together the Yin and the Yang, the male and the female, the intellect and the emotion which will give birth to the fulfillment of your goals.

Whereas a pep talk is immediate, affirmations are long-term motivators. When you read your list of goals before you go to sleep and right after you wake up, follow the reading with a tailor-made affirmation designed to attract into your life the specific conditions you desire. Affirmations like, "I am confident"; "I am enthusiastic"; " I am happy"; "I am wealthy"; "I am empowered"; "I am empowering"; "I am healthy," or "I am filled with power." The more you use affirmations, the deliberate conscious expression of positive affirming phrases, the more you'll believe them and experience their power, their impact.

This power and impact will not be discovered overnight. Many people have been affirming negatively for decades, and it may take some time to off-set these unconscious negative affirmations. With conscious effort over time you will realize the specific results you're after. Affirming your intention enables you to tap into the storehouse of all intelligence in your subconscious mind. Your affirmations will have greatest impact if stated at a time when you are relaxed, going to sleep, or prior to engaging in some leisurely activity. A great time to use deliberate affirmations is when doing some routine job like painting, wallpapering, splitting wood, mowing the lawn, gardening—activities which require little conscious thought.

One Hundred Affirmations

Here are more than one hundred affirmations for you to draw upon. They've been arranged so you can choose from the appropriate category when you want to grow and improve in this direction.

Action:

"I act as if success were inevitable"

"Today I seize the moment...I am the master of my destiny."

"I am the director in the movie of my life. Lights, camera, it's time to take action!"

Accomplishment:

"I take pride in a job well done. Accomplishment is my greatest reward. I always do more than I get paid for, so that I ultimately get paid for more than I do."

"I am a miracle worker."

Adversity:

"In any adversity, I recognize no failure, no defeat. I look instead for the seed of an equivalent benefit, and I fight on persistently toward my goal, thankful for the lesson I have learned."

"I turn adversity into advantage. I am victorious!"

Appearance:

"I'm wearing a smile; I'm always in style."

"Every day in every way I'm getting better, better, and better!"

Attitude:

"I am in charge of my attitude. I feel happy, successful and positive."

"I find what I look for: I look for the good in everyone, including myself."

"Today is the greatest day of my life, and I will live it wisely."

"Life is what you make it—I make it grand!"

Change:

"Life is change, growth is an option. I choose to blossom!"

"I adapt easily to new situations. I am flexible."

Creativity:

"I treat all problems as opportunities to be creative and as a result, my life is vastly enriched."

"I use creativity in every endeavor and thus enjoy a position of growing leadership."

"I start every job by thinking how to do it better than it has been done before."

"Thinking in terms of a better way, I always find a better way."

"I have an unusual ability to reach creative solutions to my problems. Knowing that I have this ability, my creative powers actively support my belief and I have a constant flow of new and good ideas."

"Ideas are now coming to me that will help me achieve my goals. I thankfully and gratefully accept them."

"Today I tap into my unlimited potential I am very creative."

Composure:

"I have complete composure at all times."

"I accept challenge and arguments calmly and in good spirit."

"I recognize that disagreement is an inevitable outgrowth when groups of people engage in the problem-solving process."

Decisiveness:

"I am quickly decisive in all matters, only making sure that I have complete and accurate data before acting. "

"By deciding everything quickly, I am tremendously productive."

"I make decisions quickly. I know that by deciding quickly, I make the best decisions."

"I always know what to do next."

"My decisive qualities are always awake to challenge. The more difficult the problem, the more eagerly I respond to the task, and the more my intelligence is stimulated."

Emotions:

"I contact, feel, and easily show my emotions to myself and to all other people. If I'm angry, I show it and thus release it. If I'm happy, I show this; if I'm sad, I find it easy to weep and thus dispel the sadness."

"The ability to show emotions at appropriate times is valuable, and marks me as a mature person."

"I am in complete control of my emotions and use my emotional power to achieve my goals."

Enthusiasm:

"I sizzle with enthusiasm and power. I am alive, alert, awake and enthusiastic."

"I am cheerful. Today is a great day. I celebrate it."

"I have a passion for life—I exude enthusiasm!"

"I'm riding a wave of success."

"Today my positive attitude is contagious."

"Rain or shine, sleet or snow, life is a joy wherever I go."

Energy:

"I possess an abundant supply of energy and draw upon it at will."

"I know that the more energy I apply to any task, the more I have to apply to the next task."

"I start with enthusiasm and my enthusiasm activates my energy."

"I work with inspiration and develop my sources of energy by continuous exercise."

"I find that my enthusiasm builds my energy, and my energy builds my enthusiasm."

"I possess boundless energy and I use it freely. I realize I must give some form of energy in return for everything I receive, and gladly give it, knowing that the more energy I give, the more I have to give."

"I am filled with power. I am a magnetic force attracting to me the people, things and circumstances needed for my success."

"Now is the time to recharge and take focus—my light shines brightly."

Extra Mile:

"I am in the business of going the extra mile. I do everything with a positive mental attitude and a pleasing personality. I willingly and gladly jump at the opportunity to serve people...even without compensation."

Foresight:

"I work with foresight. I have this foresight because my plans are built on ideals which maintain my enthusiasm to get things done."

Faith:

"I have complete faith and trust in Infinite Intelligence, and I know that I am being guided and assisted in achieving my goals."

"What I truly believe is what I'll achieve—my faith is my fortune."

Goals:

"My goals are high, and I reach them easily and quickly by affirming them constantly."

"I vividly visualize myself as the person I want to be and see myself enthusiastically achieving my goals."

"It is so easy and thrilling for me to concentrate all my thoughts and positive feelings on one thing...my goal!"

Gratitude:

"Today I show my appreciation. There is much to be thankful for."

"Today I make a list of things to be thankful for. I feel better already."

"My attitude of gratitude enriches my life."

Happiness:

"Wherever I am, I bring happiness with me."

"Today I give love and receive love freely. Now is the time for joy."

Health:

"I am perfectly healthy, mentally and physically, and I do all things to properly maintain my health."

"My health is my wealth; I invest wisely."

Honesty:

"I am honest with myself and therefore with everyone else."

Interest In People:

"I meet people easily and enjoy each new association."

"My deep sincerity puts people at ease and stimulates their confidence."

"I find each new personality has some unique quality which enriches my experience."

"I like people, and I radiate warmth and friendship to all. People like me!"

"I willingly and gladly cooperate with others in worthwhile teamwork."

"I like to meet in harmony with my positive-minded friends to master-mind my goals."

"I love people. I plan my activities to understand the needs of people and help them to meet those needs."

"I am friendly."

"I am tolerant of other people."

"I smile at least three times every day."

"I appreciate the uniqueness in everyone. Variety really is the spice of life."

Integrity:

"Today I do the right thing. I have peace of mind."

Laughter:

"Laughter is the best medicine. I have a healthy sense of humor."

"I can find the humor in any situation. Laughter and lightness serve me well."

Learning:

"I learn from the past in all that I do, with the power of wisdom to sharpen my view."

"Knowledge is power: Now is the time I increase my reserves."

Loyalty:

"I am loyal to all who depend on me."

Maturity:

"I am a mature person and consequently seek even greater growth within myself. I know that everyone around me is benefited by the evidence of my maturity."

"I spend my time and money wisely and with maturity. "

Memory:

"I have am an excellent memory, not only for the immediate tasks, but for all experiences that enrich my life. My memory grows better every day."

Money:

"I like money; I use it creatively and constructively. I release money with joy and it returns to me a thousand-fold."

Motivation:

"I always do things as they need to be done. I start vigorously and promptly each day on each new task. My sustained energy makes me an achiever."

"There's no excuse, it's time to produce."

"I have the energy and drive to do more than survive—I choose to flourish!"

"Today I soar to new heights; the sky is the limit."

Organization:

"I am well organized in every phase of my life."

"I organize my thoughts and emotions into a positive driving force toward my goal."

"Today I set my priorities right—I am organized."

Perseverance:

"I am easily able to persevere and finish any task I undertake."

"Every experience is a stepping stone to my greater success and higher understanding."

Persistence:

"I persistently act and move toward my goals."

"I never quit until I have reached my objective. I am a winner, and winners never quit."

Planning:

"I always plan my work. I organize my efforts today, for tomorrow, and the future."

"I work with my goals in mind. I plan ahead to get ahead."

Prosperity:

"I am always positive, prosperous-minded and filled with self-confidence."

"I have the magic touch—everything I do prospers."

"What I feel becomes real. I choose to feel prosperous."

Quality:

"I work for quality. I have the patience to do simple things perfectly and thereby strengthen my skill to do difficult things easily."

Reading:

"I read quickly and easily with great comprehension of all subject matter."

Relaxation:

"I am easily able to relax as deeply as I wish at any time. I use this ability to conserve my energy."

"I remember to take a deep breath. I feel refreshed."

"I am centered and calm in all situations. Patience is my virtue."

"I ignore negative situation which I cannot change and concentrate on positive situations in which I can succeed."

Self-confidence:

"I achieve what I set out to do. I am confident."

Self-improvement:

"I eagerly seek to improve in every phase of my life."

"I know that leaders are readers. I systematically study books and magazines which increase my earning power."

"I am a better person today than I have ever been."

"I am dynamic in my self-improvement because I am consistent in my efforts."

Self-liking:

"I like myself very much at all times. Since this thought precedes my actions, I am consistently pleased with my behavior."

Speech:

"I am an excellent speaker, well prepared, logical, and completely at ease before any group."

"I am an excellent speaker because I have knowledge of my subject and an intense desire for other people to hear it."

Success:

"I am a success."

"I am very successful in all that I do. I enjoy an abundance of all things, qualities, and conditions necessary to the happiness of myself and those around me."

" Success comes easily to me."

"I am successful in my chosen field because I'm entering this work with an enthusiasm that mounts each time I make a call or teach a class or see a client."

"I'm guided at all times to do and say the things that lead to my ultimate triumphant success."

"I'm knocking on the door to greater success."

"There are lots of reasons to fail—I choose to succeed."

Thinking:

"I think before I act."

"I control my thoughts and feelings at all times."

"I have an alert, positive mental attitude, and persistently think and act in the direction of my good and my goals."

Affirmations help build a burning desire. Affirmations fix your attention on your goals. Practice affirming as often as possible. Write out the affirmations that represent what you want to do and become. Your goals should be stretchingly believable. They should be high enough to be meaningful—worthy of your attention, interest and commitment—but small enough to be believable when you stretch your mind.

Repeat your affirmations every day until they literally become true for you. Find the ones that you think apply to the goals you have set, and repeat them with feeling.

Put them on a card in your wallet, or briefcase; tape them on your bathroom mirror, and put them on your car's sun visor. Here's the affirmation I have used for over twenty-five years:

> *"I am successful in my chosen field because I enter this work with an enthusiasm that mounts each time I make a call, teach a class, or see a client. I'm guided at all times to do and say the things that lead to my ultimate triumphant success,"*

Now, write down the affirmations you've selected from the list provided, or create personal ones of your own.

My goal-demonstrating affirmations are: _____

_____

_____

_____

_____

_____

_____

Chapter 11

Subconscious Mind

(Strategy #5)

The creative is the place where no one else has ever been. You have to leave the city of your comfort and go into the wilderness of your intuition. You can't get there by bus, only by hard work and risk and by not quite knowing what you're doing. What you'll discover will be wonderful. What you'll discover will be yourself.

—Alan Alda

In his classic book, *Think and Grow Rich*, Napoleon Hill suggests that you "read your goals each night before you go to sleep and let the unconscious, sub-conscious mind work on them as you move through the night."

Read your goals first thing in the morning to set the tempo and direction of your day so you move toward the achievement of your goals all day. These goals give our lives meaning and create a greater purpose.

Being truly turbo-charged, experiencing the thrust of the turbo-charger, requires that we accept and know that there is an invisible world beyond the five senses, something beyond the world of cause and effect.

I was working on a building project at home and couldn't figure out how to fasten the thing together. My granddaughter Alexander Michelle coaxed me onto the trampoline. We bounced, laughed, and played. My conscious mind was on play, laughter, and fun, but my subconscious mind, my unconscious mind, was working on the problem without my even knowing it.

After several minutes of play, I looked over at the shed I'd been working on, and I could see the answer clearly.

Allow time and space in your work for intuition to enter; allow spaces and places for relaxation and play, and trust your subconscious mind.

When Napoleon Hill was trying to name his book, the best name he and his publisher could come up with was *How To Make A Boodle With Your Noodle*. They weren't nuts about the title. On the eve of the deadline for the publicity of the book, Napoleon Hill said to his subconscious mind before going to sleep, "You've served me well in the past, you'll serve me well now." At 2:00 a.m., he sat up in the bed, and said, "I've got it, I've got it!" He called his publisher and said, "It's *Think and Grow Rich*"!

When you're pressed for answers, baffled for solutions, step back, rest or play, and you'll have better answers than you thought possible.

Edison was known to lock himself in his lab for days at a time. But he didn't' go without sleep when he was faced with a seemingly insurmountable obstacle in his pursuit of the answer to a problem like the creation of a practical incandescent bulb.

Edison, who had over 15,000 patents, would lie down on his couch with a heavy ball bearing in his hand. When he fell asleep and was completely relaxed, his hand would open, release the ball bearing which would fall to the floor, and awaken him. He said he often had the answer to a problem when he came to consciousness. he developed a specific strategy for the utilization of the subconscious mind. Your mind will find answers for you, too if you ask clear, demanding questions.

Act on Hunches

After I had conducted a workshop at Smoker-Craft Boats in Stayton, Oregon, I asked the Plant Manager, Jim, if he knew any of the managers in the nearby businesses. He gave me the name of a manager in the manufacturing plant down the road. Stopping there, I found that the person was no longer employed there. On a hunch, I asked the receptionist if I could see the General Manager. She said,

"I'm sorry, he's not available." I left a note and hurried off to my next appointment.

I was astounded, not long thereafter, to get a message from the General Manager saying, "I'm looking forward to meeting you." We did meet, and I'm reasonably sure it will open up an entire new market niche for us.

What I learned from this experience is the importance of acting on my hunches, disciplining myself to listen to and act upon my positive inner drives, impulses, and intuitions. I also learned that if I plant enough seeds intelligently, I will reap a harvest. There's no harvest without planting.

Follow your inner intelligence. Take positive actions around your guidance. An ounce of action is worth a ton of theory. Intelligent activity is always rewarded. Commit to your dreams.

> *"Your willingness to act is the measure of your true desire."*

Keep Your Eyes and Ears Open

LaConner, Washington, is a tourist town in tulip country that's filled with wonderful shops of all kinds. In an antique shops, I found a rare book section and started looking through some old books. I'd been looking for years for a book written in 1930 by E.T. Webb and John Morgan called *Strategies In Handling People*. It's a landmark book in practical applied psychology in leadership. I was just leaving the book section when I spotted it. I'd been looking for it for years, and there it was. Now it's in my home.

The lesson I learned is that if I know what I want and keep moving with my eyes open, I'll find what I'm after.

Decide, today, what you want. Clarify your desires, your values, your goals, and keep moving with your eyes open. The benefit you'll gain is a life full of discovery and joy, and you'll be turbocharged.

One afternoon, after spending the day at the beach, Susan told our Leadership Lab, as she was fixing dinner, her kids got in the bathtub to wash off the brine and sand. They were having a wonderful time, and she was cooking away, when she heard a still small voice inside her head say, *"Check on the kids."* She listened, she *could hear them playing, and she went on cooking. But there it was again, that still small voice saying, "Check on the kids."* She called out, "Kids, how are you doing?" They were laughing and called back, "We're having fun." Susan went on cooking. Still, she heard that still small voice, persistently saying, *"Check on the kids."* She set aside her cooking, walked into the bathroom, and found two children in the front of the tub playing and having fun. Her third child was submerged behind them, unconscious. He had turned blue. Susan grabbed the child and, in a matter of moments, had brought him back to consciousness.

Susan told us, the lesson she learned is the importance of listening to the still, small voice. "It's there to help me."

Have you ever had a hunch, heard a voice, seen a sign that caused you to take some action? Something that defied logic, science or man-made rules?

Describe the event: _____

_____

_____

_____

_____

_____

_____

_____

_____

It wasn't an accident. Trust it. Listen to your inner voice. By acting on its call, you'll be turbo-charged.

> *Sometimes you need to look reality in the eye, and deny it.*
> —Garrison Keillor

Chapter 12

Master Mind

(Strategy #6)

*What I need is someone who will help me do what I can
do.*   —Ralph Waldo Emerson

B enjamin Franklin tells in his *Autobiography* about forming a
support group early in his life. He tells how the group,
except for one contentious person, stayed together for more
than 40 years. All the members became well-known men of means.
It was the most important cause of his achievements, according to
him.

As for me, I'll never forget the winter day in 1960, SPC 4th Class
Redman opened my barracks' room door and pitched in a copy of
Think and Grow Rich. As the book bounced on my bed, he said,
"Here, Dennis, you like this kind of junk."

He knew I "liked that kind of junk," because he'd heard me playing Earl Nightingale's record, *The Strangest Secret* over and over
for weeks. I began reading the book, and I could not put it down. I
asked him if he had taken the time to read it, and he said he hadn't,
which is too bad, but I'm sure glad he passed it on to me. *Think and
Grow Rich* started me on a path of studying self-help materials
which has never ended. He helped change the course of my life.

One of the chapters in Napoleon Hill's book is titled, "The Science of the Master Mind." Though I endeavored to implement
everything I read, it took me twenty years to form my Master Mind
Group.

Finally, in 1981, I formed a Master Mind Group. My Master
Mind partners and I have been meeting on a regular basis ever since.
Maybe a part of the reason I didn't form a Master Mind Alliance
immediately was because I didn't understand how to go about it.

The purpose of this chapter is to show you *how* you can apply the profound Master Mind principal of success to turbo-charge your performance. Napoleon Hill said, "No greatness has ever been achieved without the power of the Master Mind at work."

And all wise providence has so arranged the mechanism of the mind that no single mind is complete. An alliance of two or more minds, working together in the spirit of perfect harmony, for the attainment of a definite purpose. Every leader's motto should be, "The greatest among you shall be the servant of all!"

—Napoleon Hill

Five Principals of the Master Mind

1. The Master Mind Principle is a method of applying the assets of others to whatever end you may wish to pursue through a mutually beneficial association. It is a practical medium through which you may use the experience, education and specialized knowledge of your Master Mind partners as completely as if they were your own. Their whole purpose is to build each other by sharing, accepting and encouraging each other. The group creates a positive charge that is stronger than the negative forces the individual members encounter during the week. A success support system helps its members gain more confidence. They enjoy constant, sustained support—a quality of support that builds with time.

2. There must be an alliance with a spirit of *active, perfect harmony, courage, and faith*; and a definite common objective that stimulates each mind to a degree of courage and belief that is greater than ordinary.

Active implies a sense of definiteness of purpose and planning that must be coupled with action in order to keep the Master Mind in operation.

Perfect Harmony is based upon five factors: confidence, understanding, fairness, trust and justice.

Courage is acting in spite of fear or danger. It is a mental power that derives from self-confidence, success consciousness, and the habit of controlling your thoughts.

Faith is a state of mind in which individuals clear their minds of all negative ideas and condition themselves to the inflowing of Infinite Intelligence.

3. A Master Mind Alliance stimulates each mind to move with enthusiasm, personal initiative, and imagination while enhancing the mind's intuitive abilities. For a period of time after a Master Mind meeting, there exists a sense of mental intoxication and elation due to the influx of energy from the Infinite Intelligence. You must be careful of the thoughts that are allowed to remain in your consciousness during this powerfully stimulated state.

4. This alliance, when actively applied, has the effect of synergistically connecting the subconscious sections of the minds of the Master Mind partners and gives them full access to the spiritual powers of each member.

Connecting the conscious minds of individuals is teamwork. While this may appear somewhat similar, the synergistic blending of subconscious minds is dependent upon absolute harmony and not the ordinary cooperation of teamwork.

Emerson stated, "Every institution is the lengthened shadow of one man." You can add, "and their Master Mind Group."

When subconscious minds are united in harmony with singleness of purpose, there is brought into being the most powerful influence on the face of the earth. This is the most awesome force in existence whose potentialities stagger the imagination and yet is under the control of the individuals who have a settled, harmonious, definite purpose.

5. All above-average achievement is attained through the Master Mind alliance. The fine sensitivity to the Creative Intelligence that the Master Mind creates, demands a positive mental attitude and enthusiasm. All successful individuals practice pulling down mental curtains to shut out negative influence from entering their minds. The empowering Master Mind partner believes for each other things which each would find difficult to conceive and believe for themselves.

How to Form a Master Mind Alliance

A Master Mind group is *not* established for the purpose of solving each other's problems, but rather to turn problems and goals over to the Master Mind. There are two types of Master Mind alliances: those that come into existence for business purposes and those that are personal. The relationship between a man and woman sharing love and life's experience is a personal Master Mind Alliance. Also included here are friendships, religious groups, civic and social clubs. Business alliances are formed to enhance the economic well-being of each of its members. It is to your advantage to form a Master Mind Alliance with those who bring broader experience, and will support you in all your efforts to grow and reach your goals.

The following steps are essential in forming a Master Mind Alliance:

1. *Define the Purpose.* Adopt a definite purpose to be attained by the group. Choose individual members whose education, experience and influence make them of greatest value in achieving that purpose. You may need to occasionally allow people to leave who don't possess the right talents or fall out of harmony with the purpose of the group.

2. *Determine the Benefits.* A Master Mind partner is someone with whom you meet regularly in a spirit of harmony, trust and love to take the steps into the Master Mind consciousness. They listen attentively to your requests made to the Master Mind and totally support you in becoming and achieving all that your heart desires. You must determine the benefits each member may receive and analyze the motives that each person in the group has for participation. Understanding a person's motives will enhance your ability to appeal for cooperation. Determine two or three people you'd like to invite to join your group: friends for a personal support system, or business associates or acquaintances for a business group. Qualify them with these questions:

    a) Can you trust them to keep confidences?

    b) Are they sharing, giving people?

    c) Are they success-oriented people?

    d) Are they positive-thinking people?

    e) Do they share many of your values?

    f) Do you enjoy each other?

    g) Will they see benefits to this association?

    h) Are they prompt and dependable?

When you ask them to join your group, visit each one individually, explain the plans for the group, lay the ground rules, and ask them if they would like to be included.

3. Establish the *Place and Time*. Set a definite place and time. Mondays or Fridays seem to work best—this allows you to either start or end the week with the excitement of your MasterMind meeting. Meet on a regular basis, weekly is most desirable. Be aware that resistance to the place and time may represent a lack of harmony on the part of a member. Meetings may be held in a home, place of business, restaurant, or any mutually agreeable location. Meetings should be fairly brief, thirty to ninety minutes maximum, and held to the purpose intended. Don't allow your meetings to drag on.

4. Promote *Leadership and Harmony*. It is the responsibility of the leader to see that complete trust and harmony is maintained and that action toward your goal is continuous. Rotate chairperson either weekly or monthly. You may not see or ever know your goals, much less get motivation, until you have talked them out with others. Never criticize or speak negatively about others in your group. Never argue, debate or let negative conversation develop; it'll kill the effectiveness of the whole group. Don't discuss weather, sports, politics, the economy or current events.

The Master Mind Meeting

In order to establish a consciousness of excitement, success, and expectancy, a short sharing time of specific successes is encouraged at the beginning of your meeting. Then have a time to share a progress report. Members will share reports of success, and goals achieved.

1. Discuss Reading Materials. If a book is being used as a motivational vehicle, each person shares how they have benefited after reading one chapter of the assigned self-help leadership book. (All members read the same chapter during the week and practice the principles.)

   a) Tell what you have learned.

   b) Tell how you have practiced a principle.

   c) Tell what happened to you as a result.

The leader then reminds the group of the power in the Master

Mind Alliance, a power willing to respond in a very loving, personal way when we ask.

2. Update Goals. Each person expresses his or her goal and receives the full attention and support of every other member, following which each one responds in turn with an affirmation such as, "You have the support of the Master Mind, and you will experience what you have asked for."

3. Deal with Disruptions. Any person who becomes jealous, envious, creates friction, or develops a negative mental attitude should be asked to leave at once.

Master Mind partners choose those with whom they wish to be in partnership. Before a new member can be added all existing members must agree on the admittance of the new partner. A Master Mind partner is someone to call upon when help or support is needed. Master Mind partners usually stay in close touch with each other. Knowing that support is as close as the telephone is a great comfort when you are going through difficulties. There is also joy in sharing the good news of achieved goals and success with one who understands and joins you in your spirit of gratitude. Master Mind partners listen and care.

A Master Mind partnership is a community of equals. There is a no "leader"—any of the partners may take the initiative in contacting the others regarding meeting times. However, during the Master Mind meeting itself, one person may assume the role of leading the others through the steps into the Master Mind consciousness. The leader is responsible for directing the group and keeping the attention focused.

4. Maintain Confidentiality. A Master Mind partner is someone who keeps a confidence. Because of the close nature of the Master Mind alliances, deeply personal things may sometimes be shared. The maintenance of the bond between partners is dependent on each member's ability to honor confidentiality.

5. Optimum Participation. The number of individuals in an Alliance should be governed by the magnitude of the purpose and kept to as few members as possible. Three to six people are ideal. A minimum of three members are needed for stimulation. When you go beyond six, it can be difficult to manage the coordination and harmony needed.

Five Factors of Master Mind Consciousness

Each member must affirm the desirability of achieving the following five elements:

1. Element of Desire. You must admit that you need help and you are unable to improve your own life without the aid of like-minded individuals.

2. Element of Transcendence. You must accept the belief that when two or more people come together in a spirit of perfect harmony there comes into existence a third mind, the Master Mind. This Master Mind will provide you with anything you can conceive of and believe.

3. Element of Responsibility. You are responsible for your own thinking. Furthermore, your thinking has created your present situation. You accept that your self-defeating and erroneous thinking is the cause of your problems, failures, unhappiness and fears. You know that altering your belief system and controlling your thoughts will transform your life. You are ready to have your belief system altered so your life can be changed.

4. Element of Transformation. You are ready to give up false beliefs and limitation thinking and ask to be changed. To do this, you are willing to turn your life over to the guidance of the Master Mind and understand that the transformation is taking place at unconscious levels.

5. Element of Forgiveness. You realize that unconscious resentments are projected indiscriminately onto those you work with. You now forgive and release anyone who has harmed or offended you. You also forgive yourself for any mistakes you might have made. Your mind is now open to function synergistically with your Master Mind partners.

Synergism

Webster's defines synergism as the "co-operative action of discrete agencies so that the total effect is greater than the sum of the two effects taken independently." There are three aspects to synergism in the Master Mind philosophy: *Visualization, Feeling and Commitment.*

Synergistic Visualization. The process whereby you see and believe in your mind's eye the requests that you and your partners ask of the Master Mind. Each member of the Alliance is visualizing

141

simultaneously. It is important to be positive and open-minded during the visualization process and to be as specific as possible so you and your Master Mind partners can "see" in harmony.

Synergistic Feeling. The development of such an intensity of belief that you have the same feelings you would have if the request were already fulfilled. This intensification of belief to the level of a burning desire and experiencing the joy in having attained your goal heralds the development of applied faith.

Synergistic Commitment. A three-fold agreement:

1. Each member agrees to believe in the others' ability to achieve, knowing that when they have doubts or fears, the other members of their group are believing for them.

2. Each partner is committed to living in a manner that will set a high example for others to follow and be open to the in-flow of ideas or insights from the Master Mind.

3. Each member knows with a calm assuredness that everything needed for the attainment of the goal is being provided at the right time and in the right measure.

Master Mind meeting ends on a spirit of enthusiasm, excitement and expectancy, knowing "what the mind can conceive and believe, it can achieve."

Support

January 1, 1994, was a world's record day for me. I spent the day at Lake Tahoe on the Squaw Valley ski runs—the same runs where the Winter Olympics were conducted in 1990. I'm an intermediate skier, and I tried to keep up as my sons pushed me past my limits. I took more than one tumble, and in some cases I took a little less-demanding route down. But, when I got home, knowing that I'd stretched beyond my former limitations, I felt like a winner.

If you want to grow and improve, push past old limitations, surround yourself with people who are better than your are, and then work to try to keep up with them. Build into the fabric of your life caring, supportive people. you'll achieve more of your potential by surrounding yourself with caring, supportive people—people who want the best for you, who care for you, and are willing to support you in your achievements. They will help bring out the best in you and everything you do.

Support and affirm others. It will uplift and empower you. When you affirm others, you receive more than you give. You receive empowerment.

Take a moment to affirm those around you, tell them about their strengths, their qualities of character. And when others share their goals with you ever so tentatively, affirm them, paint a picture for them of their success. You will experience then an immediate sense of upliftment. You'll be turbo-charged!

When others see it they believe it too. As you radiate miracles and real magic in your life it is contagious.

So, who will you invite to join your Master Mind Group? What qualities do they possess that can help you realize your goals?

Name: _____

Quality: _____

Name: _____

Quality: _____

Name: _____

Quality: _____

Name: _____

Quality: _____

Name: _____

Quality: _____

Name: _____

Quality: _____

Don't wait for twenty years like I did. You can gain the same sharing advantage that Ben Franklin, Thomas Edison, Harvey Firestone, Henry Ford and so many others have enjoyed. Start *Now* to put your Master Mind Alliance together.

If you can keep your head when all about you
Are losing theirs and blaming it on you.
If you can trust yourself when all men doubt you.
But make allowance for their doubting too;
If you can wait and not be tired by waiting
Or being lied about, don't deal in lies.
Or being hated don't give way to hating.
And yet don't look too good. nor talk too wise;
If you can dream—and not make dreams your master;
If you can think—and not make thoughts your aim.
If you can meet with Triumph and Disaster
And treat those two impostors just the same
If you can bear to hear the truth you've spoken
Twisted by knaves to make a trap for fools.
Or watch the things you gave your life to, broken.
And stop and build 'em up with worn-out tools;
If you can make one heap of all your winnings
And risk it on one turn of pitch-and-toss
And lose, and start again at your beginnings
And never breath a word
If you can force your heart and nerve and sinew
to serve your turn long after they are gone.
And so hold on when there is nothing in you
Except the Will which says to them: "Hold on."

—Rudyard Kipling

Chapter 13

Balance

(Strategy #7)

Life is like riding a bicycle. You don't fall off unless you stop peddling.
                                                    —Claude Pepper

When my niece arrived at my house for Thanksgiving, she asked her dad if he'd take a test ride with her in her little Honda. She said it seemed to be vibrating. My brother Bill hadn't gotten to the top of our driveway before he was 90% sure it was a bad tire. Then he and I took off for the tire store, with Michelle following in the Honda. Bill said, "Please slow down. Michelle's tire might blow at any minute."

I said, "Well, gee, she must have been driving at least sixty coming down from Seattle."

"She slowed down when she discovered something was wrong," Bill said, and then told me how Michelle came to the conclusion that something was wrong. "She'd been singing on the drive down and all of a sudden she couldn't sing because her teeth were chattering." No doubt the tire had started separating weeks ago and had become a little rougher, a little wobblier each day until it was hard to remember what a smooth ride really felt like. But she wasn't sure that something was wrong until her teeth started chattering and she couldn't sing any longer.

It's frequently that way. Things get a little out of balance, then a little more, then a little more, until we can't sing. When this happens, we need a friend to help us analyze what went wrong. So, today, take a look (with a friend) at your life. See if you can spot an area that may be a little out-of-balance (work, eating, exercising, spending, learning, friendship, resting). Take decisive action in this area. Take the necessary action you need to improve. Things will smooth out quickly, and you'll soon be singing again.

Take Time to Play

A few friends came over to celebrate Donna Lee's birthday. We talked, ate pizza, sang "Happy Birthday," and played games. I'd had a long week, had delivered two talks the day before, and was tired. I did sneak in a nap before our guests arrived, but I would have preferred to spend the evening alone. To my surprise, I had a fantastic time. We laughed and shouted. It was far more renewing, far more stimulating, than the diversion of just watching television or seeing a movie.

I need social playtime in my life, and so do you. We're social creatures. Set aside time for diversions, have fun with friends. I guarantee that with stimulating friends, you'll get a lift in your life that will give you that extra dimension needed for you to break through.

Get enough rest. A nap is not a waste of time. Often these naps are referred to as "Power Naps." Take a nap and you'll have more self-direction, you'll be more pro-active, you'll solve your problems with greater speed and ease.

David, a superintendent for a steel warehouse, told us, "In 1984, although I had been bowling for twenty-three years, I'd never bowled a perfect game. At this time of my life my goal was to bowl a perfect 300 game. I had been talking to the few people that had achieved this goal. No matter what they told me I was still unable to bowl 300. I knew that I could not advance to the next level until I had accomplished this feat.

"On December 20, 1984, when I walked into the bowling alley it was no different than any other night of bowling. What I did not know was that I was going to learn the secret of bowling a perfect game. It would come to me by accident.

"After bowling my first game of the night, I was still no closer to a perfect game. While I was waiting for the start of the second game a song popped into my head. Now, this was a song I had heard on the radio while I was driving to the bowling alley. It had a good beat, so while I bowled my second game I kept playing the song over and over in my head. Soon I had five strikes in a row, then six, now seven! As my string of strikes grew so did the importance of keeping the song in my mind.

"After rolling my eighth strike in a row my mind tried to take over the game. It reminded me that I had rolled eight strikes in a row before, but *never* nine. I countered this added pressure by putting the song back into my mind. Armed with the song, not only was I able to roll the ninth strike, but it seemed easy to do! It was so easy I was ready to bowl the tenth frame. However, I had to wait my turn. When my turn came up I felt ready as I stepped up to the ball return.

"As I reached for my bowling ball I suddenly realized that things had changed. No longer was there any noise of pins being knocked down. No one else was up and bowling. The biggest thing that I noticed was the quiet that had come over the bowling alley. It seemed that everyone in the bowling alley was standing behind me waiting to see me perform.

"All I had to do was roll three strikes in a row to reach my goal. Three strikes in a row with everyone watching me. Was there enough power in the song to carry me to my goal?

"It was all I had, so I put it back into my mind. As I reached for my ball, I noticed that my hands were shaking. As I stepped up onto the approach, not only could I hear my heart pounding, but I could feel it up in my throat. Somehow I was able to roll strikes ten, eleven and twelve. Of course, everyone came down and shook my hand and patted me on the back.

"I cannot put into words what it felt like to finally roll a 300 game.

"Two years later I bowled a second 300 game. Two years after that I bowled my third. I learned that my mind had put limitations on what I was able to do. Physically I had been ready for a long time. Mentally, I had not been prepared. By taking my mind off the game, with the help of a song, I was able to let my body do the work and not my mind. I was never able to use a song to bowl a good game after that. However that one time that it happened taught me what no one else could teach me.

"I have now been bowling for thirty-two years. Each year I make new goals. I don't always reach them, but with the new knowledge I have I know that it is just a matter of time before I do. I have gone to even higher levels since that first 300 game. I will never forget that it started with a song."

So today, set your stretching goals with your conscious mind, then go into action with a song on your mind. Don't worry who is watching, what they might say, how you might look, find the calm in the middle of the storm and you will perform with excellence and grace.

When I got home on Saturday from work I thought would only take a few hours, it was already dark. I thought I'd do some fooling around in the garage until it was time for dinner, but Donna Lee said, "How about fooling around with me?"

It seems like I need someone to remind me to stop. For our lives to be fully functional, we must search for order, harmony, balance, intelligence, growth, attraction, and fulfillment. Your personal master plan must include the following elements if you wish to be completely fulfilled: the physical side of your life; your mental and intellectual side; your emotional nature; your social side; your moral and ethical side; and your spiritual relationship to God. These six basic elements must be present in your life if you are to have order, balance, harmony, growth, and fulfillment in your future life.

So, take time out to fool around. It may be the high point of your day, and it will help you stay in balance.

Our 22-year-old son Loren who lives in Los Angeles paid us a surprise visit. I had just returned from teaching a class in Bellevue, Washington, and was walking down Concourse C at the Seattle airport when I heard his voice. Wow, what a surprise! We had a wonderful visit, however brief. He'd also come to surprise his girlfriend. As I reflected on the experience, I was reminded of what my true values are—what's really important to *me*.

Friday afternoon, I took off from work a little early to take our four-year-old granddaughter Alex to Discovery Zone. We swam in a bath of red and blue and green plastic balls. We climbed blue mountains. We climbed through what seemed to be miles of plastic tunnels. What a wonderful place to play and have fun. I've always worked long hours, but I like to think that I've been able to maintain my values and some balance at the same time. By Friday afternoon, I'm usually a little tired, and feel the need to become sedentary, and I sometimes go to bed early. After playing with Alex for just a few minutes, I felt alive, alert, and fully awake.

The previous Friday, when I got home I was real tired. It had been a long week, and I wanted to go to bed and stay there, but I had a 7:00 appointment for a ski lesson on the indoor ski ramp. I did take a short nap, then got up to keep my commitment. Since this was my first time—a world's record for me—I was a little apprehensive. But I enjoyed the lesson, learned a lot and made some real progress. I'm excited about my next visit. I left feeling exhilarated, invigorated, alive.

It's important to schedule in recreational activities. If you're like me, you may need the discipline of appointments to maintain your recreational activities. Don't leave your enjoyment—your re-creation—up to chance. Schedule it in, maybe with a friend. Make an appointment to play. Time you enjoy wasting isn't wasted time. Play is energizing.

Are you taking the time to play? Sort out your values and redouble your commitment to all of them and be sure you're giving quality time to all of your true values. Become involved in energizing play. Involve yourself beyond what you feel are your limits, and you'll find that you have more energy—a reserve source of energy you didn't know was yours. You'll have a more centered life, more balance, and this balance and centeredness will help you be turbocharged.

Answer the following questions:

I can build greater balance into my life by:_____

_____

_____

_____

_____

_____

_____

Here's the action I will take today to restore balance and calm to
my life: _____

_____

_____

_____

_____

_____

Chapter 14

Planning

(Strategy #8)

The great thing in this world is not so much where we are, but in what direction we are moving.
—Oliver Wendell Holmes

A determined lady at a dinner party spotted someone across the floor and began to wind her way through the audience. When she arrived at the other side of the room, she looked up at the attractive man, introduced herself and said, "I just had to say 'Hello' to you." This made the man a little ill at ease.

Not knowing how to respond, he said, "Why?"

She said, "Because you look exactly like my fifth husband."

Not sure of the appropriate response, he said "Oh, how many times have you been married?"

Her response: "Four."

Now, this is a woman who clearly set her sights. If you are to reach your potential, to experience the turbo-charged life, you first must know exactly where you're going, have a plan, and go into action.

Plan Ahead

It was after dinner and a couple were sitting in the family room when the husband put to the wife a very awkward question. He said, "If I die will you remarry?"

His wife avoided his question by responding with, "Wasn't that a great dinner?"

He said, "No, really. If I die first will you remarry?"

"Did you enjoy the dessert?" she said.

Not to be side-tracked, he said, "Seriously, now. If I die will you remarry?"

"I wonder what's on TV," she said.

But he persisted. "Come on! I want to know! Will you remarry?"

Finally, pushed to the limit, she responded by saying, "I suppose so."

He'd suspected she felt that way and said, "Oh, you will? Will he sleep upstairs in our bed?"

"Well, I suppose he would," she said.

"Well," the husband asked, "would he drive my car?"

"Well, I suppose so," she answered again."

"Okay, well," the husband next wondered, "would he use my golf clubs?"

"Heavens no," she replied, "he's left-handed."

This woman had a plan, an alternate strategy already in mind. For you to reach your goals, you need to have a plan and alternate strategies in mind. Planning helps us remain flexible.

True optimists are seldom surprised by trouble. Rather, they plan ahead to avoid bad situations. They ask discriminating questions. Being optimistic certainly doesn't mean saying yes to everyone and everything. It means enlightened self-interest.

Every morning, I dress for my most important meeting of the day, and on this particular day my most important meeting was with a local college accreditation council. I would be talking to them about accrediting our Leadership Lab. I'd been told in advance that the Head of the Department was not in favor of accrediting the program, so I wanted to be prepared, and I was. I had handouts for all four members of the evaluation committee. I'd prepared an agenda of what I thought should be covered.

The evaluation went extremely well. I not only got what I was after, they began to suggest other ways they could actually send people to us. They're planning to send some of their faculty through our training.

The lesson I learned from this experience is the importance of not pre-judging but instead pre-planning and preparing.

Prepare for every important event of the day, week, month, quarter and year. Begin with the end in mind. Decide in advance what outcomes you're after, then prepare backward right down to the clothes you wear. You'll get more of the results you're after more of the time. As you're planning, setting your direction, deciding what you want to do, what you want to be, and what you want to have, begin with the end in mind. What do you want your year to be like? What kind of job do you want to be doing? What kind of relationship, what kind of car, where do you want to be living? Now, decide how you'll get there—complete directions, plan all the way, begin with the end in mind. This planning, this picture, this complete direction in your mind will build your confidence. One hour in preparation could save you days of execution. This thorough and advanced preparation will help you be turbo-charged.

There's an on-going debate among many about which is the most important: the goal or the plan. Well, there's no question whatsoever in my mind that what's most important is the goal, clearly defined. A goal without a strategic plan will probably never be achieved. Certainly, a goal without action will not be achieved. At the beginning of all meaningful efforts and activities is a clearly defined goal, and then the plan that follows.

Decide for Yourself

The quality of your life and success in your career will depend more on the quality of your decisions than on any other single factor. Most of the decisions we make seem unimportant on the surface: What tie shall I wear this morning? What will I do tonight? What book shall I read? Which program shall I watch on TV? What do I want for lunch? Yet these little decisions, piled one on another, dramatically color the quality of our lives.

The average person has a difficult time making almost any decision that falls out of the pattern of habit. We go on "automatic" and make decisions without thinking of consequences, and then we wonder why nothing is happening in our lives.

There is a great temptation to abdicate decision-making to someone else: a boss, a supportive spouse, a friend, the persuasive salesperson on TV. Why? It's easy and we can blame them if it doesn't turn out right. Well, this may seem to be a "safe" way to live; the truth is, it's a powerless, impoverished, and negative way to live.

It's time to wake up and take control. You can become conscious of your decisions and *choose* what you do. When decisions are made based on the goal to improve the quality of your life, you will become successful and vital. Start with the little decisions you make without thinking. Does that tie *really* reflect you as you as you want to be? Do you eat lunch in the atmosphere you enjoy, and what kind of food do you put into your body? Is that book nourishing your mind?

When you are willing to take responsibility for your decisions, you will experience a surge of energy and power. The quality of your life and the success of your career will improve in direct proportion to the decisions you make thoughtfully and considerately.

> *Solve it. Solve it quickly, solve it right or wrong, If you solve it wrong. it will come back and slap you in the face, and then you can solve it right. Lying dead in the water and doing nothing is a comfortable alternative because it is without risk, but it is an absolutely fatal way to manage a business.*
>
> —Thomas J. Watson, Jr.

Make a List

I looked at the list laying on the workbench of my garage. Almost everything was checked off. Boy, that felt good. I'd been thinking about doing several other things for weeks but had never placed them on a list. I know that I do many things without ever having to first write them down on a list. I'm equally sure that many of the things that should be prioritized are left undone, and I end up spending my time on less important things. What's more, if I haven't taken a moment to plan ahead, to make a list, I don't get the full sense of accomplishment, achievement, reinforcement, and self-esteem. It's only if it is on a list to begin with that I get the full value that I experience from checking it off my list.

What major achievements do you want to accomplish this week? Write them down. Make a list. Share your list with others. Check things off as the week progresses. I guarantee that you will accomplish more this week by doing this than you will accomplish by just taking life as it comes, by being reactive. You'll discover, as you check items off your list, a significantly reinforced self-esteem. You'll feel better about yourself and your accomplishments. You'll be motivated to greater accomplishments through the process.

As a teenager, Thomas Edison sold newspapers. He made a habit of turning chance circumstance to his own benefit. He had a stubborn streak that made him refuse to be deterred, and he was relentless in making as much money as possible.

When he sold newspapers on the railroad lines, Thomas had to estimate how many papers he would sell on a given day because his leftover inventory ate into his profits. In order to minimize his risks, he worked out a deal so he could see the main news story before it went to print.

In 1862, he saw the opportunity to make a great profit on a sensational event regarding the Civil War. He telegraphed the news down the line so that, when he arrived, mobs of buyers were waiting to obtain the details from his newspaper. Edison had stocked enough, sold them all, and reaped the benefits. Now that's planning ahead.

I drove back to the office one night, after going home for a dinner break. I didn't want to; I was tired, and inertia had set in after dinner and a little television; but I'd planned ahead to do it, told some others that I was going to be doing it, and I'd enlisted some support people to come back in to work with me. We got back to the office at around 7:30 and left at about 9:00. We completed some filing, some organization, some clean-up work that had been hanging over my head for months. I felt empowered, I felt confident, I felt proud of myself.

Making prior plans and keeping the commitment to do those little, extra things that need to be done will help improve your effectiveness. Set aside a few minutes to organize and to plan, then commit to do it, and enlist help, if necessary. Once you've made a commitment, follow through. You'll feel better about yourself, you'll be empowered, you'll be more confident, and you'll be turbocharged.

If you have built castles in the air, your work need not be lost; that is where they should be. Now put foundations under them.

—Henry David Thoreau

Chapter 15

Action

(Strategy #9)

The genius that dazzles most men's eyes is simply hard work in disguise. —Thomas Alva Edison

A commitment is no good unless you carry it out. Carrying it out involves a four letter word that many people regard as obscene. That word is "work." Let's be clear on this: working hard, by itself, will not do it. Working smart, by itself, will not do it. You must learn to work both hard and smart. Your willingness to act is the measure of your true desires.

When I turned on my car radio, I pushed the selection button and my radio went right to my favorite drive-time station. This may be something you take for granted in your car, and you may be thinking, "Big deal." However, I've driven my Porsche 120,000 miles over the past nine years, and although I love my car, having to manually tune the radio has been a real bore. I've talked about replacing it for years, and I finally did it.

When I tried to install the radio, I saw a lot of "spaghetti" under the dash. Before long, the whole car looked like a wreck inside. At more than one point along the way, I felt overwhelmed, confused, and discouraged, but I just kept pushing and pulling one wire at a time, looking for the little missing screws, fuses, and, finally, I had it all together. It looks like original equipment, and it sounds great.

The inertia that held me back for so many years was based largely on fear, which was rooted in a lack of information. When I go into action (with persistence), however, my fear is dispelled, and I get results.

Now, I'd like you to think of some little job, some little goal you've been postponing. Act on it, today. Action will dispel your fears. And, when others see your results, the words they say will be music to your ears.

> *Thinking will not overcome fear, but action will.*
> —W. Clement Stone

Be Cheerful

Cheerfulness is something you have much more control over than happiness. You can choose to behave cheerfully in dispiriting circumstances, in part to sustain your own strength, in part as an act of courtesy to others. Acting cheerful, you'll find that you've at the same time made yourself feel happier. Act "as if" and the feelings will follow! Act as if it is impossible to fail. Don't be tentative, have courage, have confidence, and go into action.

> *I couldn't wait for success—so I went ahead without it.*
> —Jonathan Winters

Putting on a sad face, or a happy face, produces the feeling that the expression represents, according to scientists. Dr. Paul Ekman has been studying facial expressions for years and has confirmed the ideas set forth more than a century ago by Charles Darwin and William James. Dr. Ekman and other modern researchers have verified that facial expressions can influence mood and cause emotion by affecting the temperature of blood flowing to the brain. So, smile, and you'll feel better.

Decide, today, where you need to apply enthusiasm to your life, then go into action. People will watch you in amazement, and you will be turbo-charged.

Sam, the general superintendent of a painting contractor, told our Leadership Lab that when his dad, the owner of the company, left for a short vacation, he decided to apply five-times more enthusiasm to cleaning out the graveyard of old paint at his company. Two garage sales, a half-a-ton of junk iron and $400 later, things were cleaned out—things which have been hanging around, in some cases, for ten years. How did Dad react when he returned from his vacation? Dad loved it.

How about you? Where can you exercise more leadership with love and enthusiasm? It will take a ton off your load, and it'll put money in your pocket.

> *My grandfather once told me that there are two kinds of people: Those who do the work, and those who take the credit. He told me to try to be in the first group; there was less competition there.* —Indira Gandhi

Watching the All-Star basketball game two years ago, I was impressed by the precision, the orchestration, and the great athletes. Magic Erving Johnson played like he had eyes in the back of his head. But more important than that, he played like he loved what he was doing. Certainly, he earned the Most Valuable Player Award. Here's a man who has contracted the most dreaded disease of our age, a disease like leprosy of Biblical times. And still he played with love. His willingness to give credit to others was inspirational to me. In an interview, after the game, he said, "I just loved being back on the floor, getting knocked around."

Decide now to play full out with love. Set aside for one week any sense of doom or gloom. Set aside any parts of your job that you don't like and give full attention to the parts of your life and job that you do like? Fall in love again. Love is a decision.

When the week is over, and you've completed your work with love, you too may find you were chosen as the Most Valuable Player.

Do the Right Thing

Robin Hood is a thoroughly entertaining movie. All the elements of romantic love, devotion, humor, indignation, and honor mark the film, which is filled with terms of nobility like "Lord," "King," "Your Lordship," "Your Grace," and so on. My favorite line in the movie was when Robin Hood was getting reacquainted with Marian, and he said, "Nobility doesn't come by birth, but by the acts of men."

Our acts determine our character and stature, in both our eyes and the eyes of others. Each of us through our actions can raise our stature at any moment.

Act like a king or a queen. Don't put on airs, but walk with grace and dignity. Honor yourself, and you'll earn the honor of others.

In the movie *What About Bob,* Bob is so paranoid that he is afraid to leave his apartment, afraid to get on an elevator. He is so afraid of germs, he must clean it with tissues before he can touch a door handle. He's saved by the wisdom and advice of his psychiatrist, who has written a book entitled *Baby Steps* in which the psychiatrist advises taking baby steps through one's fears. The movie's a roaring spoof, but the advice is sound. If it seems that fear is holding you back as you contemplate your goals, all you really need to do is formulate your goals and take action with baby steps toward them.

Are you clear about your goals? Why not take one, two or three baby steps toward them, today, then reflect on your successes? Your future depends on your actions—on what you do *today*. Welcome your obstacles: they provide the jolt that comes when you overcome them.

> *Work banishes those three great evils: boredom, vice, and poverty.*
> —Voltaire

Isaac Asimov made his transition to the next world at age 72. Isaac Asimov was the author of nearly 500 books and 400 articles. Called "The Writing Machine," he once said to an interviewer, "I'm afraid to die and let my brain decay, but I don't have to worry because there has never been an idea in my mind that I haven't put down on paper."

Asked, "What would you do if the doctors told you, that you only had six months to live?" Asimov responded, "Type faster." This from the winner of the Hugo Award in 1966, holder of fourteen honorary degrees, and the author of ten books a year after serious heart surgery.

The lesson I learned as I reflected on Isaac Asimov's life is the importance of finding and *doing* something that I love, and putting every idea I have into action.

Find a part of your life and your work that you love, and put every idea you have into action. You'll be alive all your life, and you'll stimulate others to lead a fuller life as well.

> *If you're not succeeding at the level you'd like to succeed, my best advice to you is to double your rate of failure.*
> —Henry Ford

Establish Patterns

Habits are learned from *actions*. When you do something continuously, repeating the action over and over, it becomes a habit. A habit is something we can do without thinking. It would be hard to drive a car, type a letter, or tie your shoes if you had to stop and think about every step. Habit enables you to push in the clutch, align your fingers to the correct keys, or lace with error-free accuracy. Strong habits become automatic and require little or no thought.

A habit is much different than an instinct. An instinct is behavior that is inborn, while a habit is behavior that is learned. A stimulus, or something that starts an action, must be present each time a habit is carried out. Psychologists say that you will learn a habit only if it benefits you in some way, at least initially. If the habit satisfies a need, you will tend to keep it. When a habit becomes unpleasant, you can break it, although the more ingrained it is the harder it is to break. You may have the habit of eating a piece of coffee cake each mid-morning because of the pleasure it gives. You can break the habit if you decide that it is adding unwanted weight. This habit may have become ingrained as a type of reward or reinforcement. It can be broken by replacing it with another reward: the pleasure you get when you see yourself looking more fit, for example.

> *Life is like music, it must be composed by ear, feeling, and instinct.*
> —Samuel Butler

In studying habits, psychologists have ingrained certain habits in rats and then cut their nervous systems at many points. Despite the cuts, the rats continued to perform their habituated acts. The experiment suggests that the learning of habits does not depend on specific nerve connections and does not occur only in particular parts of the brain. What happens in the brain when we learn habits is still a mystery.

Some habits are more than simple motor acts. Many of them require thoughts and attitudes. Neat appearance and pleasant manners are considered good habits. Most habits begin as actions that a person is aware of. The more we perform the action, the easier it becomes.

Habits play an important part in human behavior. People tend to continue doing what they are used to doing as long as they possibly can.

Habits can be "good" or "bad," constructive or destructive. Changing or modifying habits involves a re-patterning of behavior, establishing patterns for success by re-enforcing desired actions.

> *Always do your best. What you plant now, you will harvest later.*
> —Og Mandino

Establish patterns that project a self-confident image. If you:

- act as if you like yourself;
- show genuine interest in others;
- walk tall and stand straight;
- hold your chin up;
- look people in the eye;
- maintain good posture at all times;
- speak up and talk directly;
- listen attentively;
- take pride in the way you dress and in your personal appearance;

you will establish the habit of projecting a self-confident image, and you'll be turbo-charged.

Procrastination and indecision affect the way you feel about yourself and the image you project. They get in the way of goal attainment. Sometimes a poor decision is better than no decision at all, because you can take action to correct a poor decision, whereas indecision stymies action altogether.

If you have the habit of procrastination, take some action today. Use baby steps, if necessary, by choosing an area where the consequences of your action are minimal. For example, if you habitually have trouble deciding what to order when you go to a restaurant, decide beforehand or even arbitrarily, then take immediate action.

In the past, I have procrastinated about _____

_____

_____

_____

_____

The goal this indecision prevents me from attaining is _____

_____

_____

_____

_____

The action I'll take to stop this procrastination is _____

_____

_____

_____

_____

As the ads for Nike say: "Just do it!"

Choose

The choices we make each day of the week.
The paths that we take, the goals that we seek.
The kind of person we one day will be
Is daily determined by you and me.
Each thought that we think, each word that we say
Affect our tomorrows in some strange way.
Each task that we finish, if it's well done.
Prepares us to tackle a bigger one.
For each of us has a talent or two.
A chance to make good on the jobs we do;
A measure of time to squander or use
is given to us—it's our job to choose.

Chapter 16

Positive Passion

(Strategy #10)

Never allow your energy or enthusiasm to be dampened
by the discouragements that must inevitable come.
                              —James Whitcomb Riley

Leadership Lab participants are asked to speak for twenty seconds about anything they are positively passionate about. Brenda at first said, "I'm not positively passionate about anything." We talked a little bit, but she insisted. "Larry, I'm really *not* passionate about anything."

I know there was a time in her life when she was passionate about butterflies, spiders, ice cream cones, Ferris wheels, snowflakes and kittens. Brenda feels her parents turned off that sparkle, spontaneity, positive joy, and passion. Life without passion is like hot-dogs without mustard, like popcorn without butter. And, to tell the truth, I'm a little tired of adults, supposedly mature adults, blaming their parents for stifling them. Instead of assigning blame for something that's missing, take action to acquire it. If you want to be positively passionate and gain all that life has available to you, take Shakespeare's suggestion and "Assume a virtue, though you have it not."

Turn it on, fake it, act it out, do whatever is necessary to assume that virtue you feel is not yours. You can be joyous. You can be passionate. Why aren't you? Frankly, most of us are worried about what other people will think. What difference does it make what "they" think? Trying to conform to the expectations of others will squelch you, turn you off, drive out your passion and drive out your joy.

So, turn on your joy, today. Find something to celebrate (a drop of rainwater, a sunset, a rainbow, a kiss, a blade of green grass). Be positively passionate about your job, about your customers, and you'll be turbo-charged.

> *I celebrate myself, and sing myself,*
> *And what I assume, you shall assume,*
> *For every atom belonging to me as good belongs to you.*
> —Walt Whitman

Here is an affirmation I have repeated hundreds of times: *"I fairly sizzle with zeal and enthusiasm and spring forth with a mighty faith to do the things that ought to be done by me."* Charles Filmore wrote this affirmation when he was 93 years old—it is not too late for you to turn up and on your zeal, your positive passion.

Start Fresh

I recently conducted a Turbo Sales Systems Workshop for the first time in months, maybe years. There was a period in my life when I conducted half-a-dozen of these sales workshops a week. At some point along the way, I seemed to burn out. In fact, I wasn't looking forward to doing the workshop this time, but as I conducted the sales meeting I discovered that I enjoyed it, I loved it. It was a lot of fun, and I was effective. I was fresh, and I was able to make some strong points in a way that was credible and impacting.

Just because you may have gone stale or flat on something in your life at some point in the past, doesn't mean that you shouldn't return or revisit the activity. Build some breathing space into your life, and if there's something you used to enjoy doing but haven't done for a while, dust it off, get it out again. You'll find that some of the freshness that was once there has returned, and it'll be just like doing it for the first time. And the knowledge that you're still very good at doing something you maybe haven't done for a while will remind you of all of your strengths and skills and abilities and capabilities, and this awareness will turbo-charge you.

I was riding on the shuttle bus from the parking lot to the Portland airport terminal, and the bus was packed with subdued, mundane, almost sedated riders, except for two wonderful, alive, warm, enthusiastic joy-filled people. They were turned on. They were excited by everything, even the lights and arrows, and when we arrived at the airport they were all pumped up. As you may have guessed, they were about ten years old.

Why do we get turned off? Why do we let ourselves go to sleep just because we've had an experience before? If you permit yourself to die just because you've had an experience once before, if you lose your excitement, your zest, your joy, then life itself has been drained from you.

Find a way, today, to discover something new, to find another dimension to the things you've been doing. Don't let routine become boredom. Find new ways to experience old things and you'll gain a new life, a child-like spontaneity and enthusiasm like what I saw in the youngsters on the bus. And this spontaneity and joy will help you be turbo-charged.

> *There is no duty we so much underrate as the duty of*
> *being happy.*   Robert Louis Stevenson

At a wedding, we sat down up front and observed the guests, from the blue-haired punker to the man in the $700 suit. We witnessed a range of human emotion, including fear, joy, and love. As we sat in the open garden setting, waiting for the wedding to begin (do all weddings start late?), I noticed how creative some people can be in their attempts to sit in the last row.

Some young men went to pick up extra chairs, although there was plenty of seating, and sat off at an angle and leaned back—away from the group. This is the body language of disassociation, of separation and non-participation. There's nothing wrong with observing life, but some people spend their life watching it pass them by.

It didn't surprise me when the reclusive single guys I had noticed shied away from the traditional toss of the garter. Although the ladies were eager enough to gather together for the toss of the bouquet, it didn't surprise me when the music started that less than 15% of the guests were dancing.

To get more out of life, to feel better about yourself, to experience the richness of life, lean into it. Sit up front, take a chance, try to catch the garter, dance. As you lean forward, you'll find momentum will take over, and you'll move faster and further. You will be turbo-charged.

When Dave was fourteen, he had a paper route. One of his customers had an old Model-A Ford in the garage. Dave negotiated with the customer to buy the automobile for $100. There was only one problem. Dave couldn't tell his parents. Another customer had a garage, so Dave negotiated to rent it for five dollars a month. Can you imagine the enthusiasm this fourteen-year-old boy generated as he drove his polished Model-A up and down the rented driveway?

Emerson spoke a deeper truth than most people recognize when he said, "Nothing great was ever achieved without enthusiasm." He understood that enthusiasm gives quality to every word we speak, to every task we set our hands on. What about you? What do you passionately want? Whether it's a new Corvette or a restored Model A, a country house or the opportunity to run for public office, follow your passion. Don't lower your standard of living by lowering your positive passion.

Turn up your heart light. Put as much passion in your goals as a young boy's dream, and you'll soon take possession of your passion.

Enthusiasm must be nourished with new actions, new aspirations, new efforts, new vision. If you want to turn hours into minutes, renew your enthusiasm.

Papyrus

At the graduation ceremony following a long and arduous Seattle Leadership Lab, Mike presented me with a walking stick to support me in my goal of successfully completing the Portland-to-Coast walk. This walking stick had been given to him by his dad many years ago, and was brought to the United States from Scotland by his grandfather. What a wonderful gift, truly a gift of the heart.

The lesson I learned from this experience is when I give the best from my heart to those who count on me, they'll respond from their hearts.

Be positively passionate. Give the best you can, today, from your heart in spite of detractors, cynics or skeptics. In turn, you'll receive a gift of the heart when it counts the most, when you need it most, in support of your goals and objectives, and you will be turbo-charged.

The pleasure of love is in loving. We are happier in the passion we feel than in that which we excite.

LaRochefoucald

Your project for this week is to purposefully change an attitude or a habit. By now you have been doing some good, sound thinking about your attitudes, and you should have begun to make a plan for changing them.

List all the attitudes you are going to change, and then write down what you are going to *do* about each one of these attitudes. However, it is not possible to do everything at once, and you won't do a good job if you try to change them all at one time. Choose just one attitude, and during the coming week, go all out to change it.

The attitude or habit I'll change is: _____

_____

_____

Now that you've decided, follow these guidelines:

1. *Start now!* If it is worthwhile, now is the time.

2. *Sell yourself.* Sell yourself on the advantages to be gained, on what the new attitude will do for you. Think it through. Become enthusiastic about it. Let both barrels go!

3. *Provide a substitute attitude or habit* (usually the opposite of the one you want to change). If you want to change a critical attitude, when you feel the urge to criticize, start sincerely praising. Look for the good. It's there! To break the habit of indecision, make a decision immediately. You will be ahead even if it's wrong. Wrong or right is not important. Indecision eats away and destroys us from the inside. Decision making builds character and gives us strength and power. If you want to break a habit of holding back, simply give. Remember, givers gain.

4. *Make it hard to retreat.* Make it so you will "lose face" if you retreat. Get some of your team in on the habit you are breaking. Agree to pay them money every time you don't "come through."

It may cost you, but you will break the habit or attitude. You will be the winner, too! Tell your manager, your spouse, or even better, your children—they'll remind you. In his book, *The Blackmail Diet*, John Bear describes making out a $10,000 check to the American Nazi Party, a group he abhors, and instructing his attorney to forward the check if he failed to lose fifty pounds by a certain date. You can be sure he lost the weight.

5. *Constantly remind yourself.* Write notes to yourself and put them in all your pockets. Put a red dot on your watch at the five o'clock position to remind yourself to be five time (5x) more enthusiastic about the new attitude you have chosen. Put notes on your mirrors, in your bedroom, bathroom, office or kitchen. Write letters to yourself, mail them, and then read them!

6. *Stay with it until the new habit is yours.* Do you recall when you learned to drive a car? It didn't take long. Why? Because you kept at it. Habits will take you up, or they will take you down. Attitudes and habits can bring you the wonderful things of life or they can dish out a mighty skimpy diet. Only you can decide what they will do for you. Attitudes and habits are standing ready and willing to go into action at your command!

Now write down your plan for changing the habit or attitude you've chosen to change. What specific steps will you take?

1. _____

2. _____

3. _____

4. _____

5. _____

6. _____

Chapter 17

Serendipity

(Strategy #11)

Webster defines serendipity as "The gift of finding valuable or agreeable things not sought for," but serendipity implies more than sheer accident. The Scottish pathologist Alexander Fleming, while studying bacteria, noticed that some of the bacteria wouldn't grow and, instead, kept dying. Many other scientists observed this, too, but Fleming was more aware of what he was seeing and took the exploration further. As a result of his efforts, he discovered penicillin. He was not searching for penicillin, but that's what he found. Others had seen mold go bad and stopped dead in their tracks. Fleming was better able to use his faculty of observation, noticing what happened along the way, and took advantage of serendipity.

Donna Lee went to the Kenny Loggins' concert at the Arlene Schnitzer Concert Hall with a group of friends. After the concert, they all wanted to go out for dessert. First, they went to The Metro Cafe, only it was about to close. Then they tried Humphrey Yogurt's, but it was also closing. As Donna was telling me this story, I was surprised that the group didn't just give up, but they chose instead to try the Heathman Hotel, where they were seated.

As they were checking out the desserts, in walked Kenny Loggins! Meeting the star and shaking his hand was the creme-de-la-creme, the highlight of their evening. Had they given up after one or two tries, they never would have had the real dessert. If they had said, "Well, it must be a sign. We're supposed to lose weight." If they had said, "I guess this is an indication that this is not for us," they would have missed the main event of the evening.

Persist in the pursuit of your goals. Don't try once, don't try twice—persist. You'll experience serendipity, a fortuitous experience. And these fortuitous, serendipitous experiences will help you be turbo-charged.

In old Ceylon, now Sri Lanka, lived the three princes of Serendip. According to legend, they never seemed to reach their goals, and even thought their goals alluded them, but they were always discovering, by chance or by sagacity, things they did not seek. They were more than rewarded by accidental occurrences. These "fortunate accidents" occur more often to goal-striving people than to people without clearly defined goals.

The Princes from Serendip were on their own personal quest, so the secret is to have a goal, a quest. For serendipity to work you must be questing and in your quest you must have great expectations. And you must believe, as the Princes of Serendip believed, that an unseen power will guide you to a better place than you can guide yourself.

Joseph Henry, the great 19th century physicist, wrote: *"The seeds of great discovery are constantly floating around us, but they only take root in minds well prepared to receive them."* You can become more conscious of the serendipitous experiences that flow into your life. You can take advantage of them, gain more value from them, utilize the experiences when they occur, and further expand the frequency of their occurrences. But serendipity can occur only when the person who sees some "lucky accident" also has the knowledge, intuition or inspiration to recognize its significant."

Focus on a goal, then expand your focus. Expect surprises. Focus on expecting, anticipating the miracle of experiencing more than you've thought—better than what you went out to seek—richer than your dreams.

Your intention creates a reality. If your intention is to experience the magic of serendipity, if you are also resolved to achieve your goals and are open to more and better than what you're pursuing, you'll realize more than your goals.

To be open to serendipity is to become more childlike in your expectations. I watched my four-year-old granddaughter ski down Squaw Valley Mountain. Her mom and dad were there to help support her. She laughed heartily when she hit a little bump, and when she fell down she couldn't wait to get up and try it again. Her enthusiasm, confidence, and joy at the unexpected occurrence were contagious.

If you want to experience more joy in life, become more childlike. Set aside any prejudice about what you can and can't do, and throw yourself into new activities. Let what happens happen. This can lead you on the road to serendipity. Explore new, uncharted waters. Set aside the "could's" and "couldn't's," the "never's" and "don't's," the "won't's" and "can't's." Be willing to accept the help of others. Expect to fall down when you're trying new things. Don't expect perfection when you're exploring new territory. Accept what is given to you, and recognize its significance.

Embrace Synchronicities

I recently met the new president of a national machine tool company. After a few pleasantries, I began to answer his unspoken questions: "Who are you? What have you done?" And, most important of all, "What can you do for me?" I generally answer these unspoken questions by telling success stories. I began to tell him one I felt he could easily relate to: it was about Mike.

"Oh, Mike," he said. "He's a neighbor of mine."

What a coincidence! The success story I'd chosen just happened to feature his neighbor. I learned that his son wrestles with Mike's son. Another wonderful coincidence. A coincidence occurs when one incident intersects another incident. We sometimes refer to coincidences as "luck," but they are really synchronous events, the intersection in time of separate occurrences resulting in serendipity.

If you would like to have more "luck" in your life, more happy coincidences, then engage in more incidents, more activities. Play in traffic. The more engaged you are, the more involved you are, the more active you are, the more happy coincidences you will discover. Serendipity will occur in your life. People will look at you and they'll say, "Boy, are you lucky," and you'll be turbo-charged.

Loren was really disappointed when the apartment on which he'd put down a deposit was mistakenly given to another renter. He was shown a different apartment in the same building. It was dirty and there were cockroaches everywhere, which led him to believe the apartment he'd lost might have also been infested.

Loren took a contemplative drive to a nearby neighborhood, to think over his next move. As he drove along, he happened upon a "for rent" sign in front of a small bungalow, a charming place with a little yard and a white picket fence. Loren's disappointment led to a "lucky" drive that provided the opportunity for something better to enter his life. He took the place on the spot.

Be clear about your goals, commit to and work toward these goals, but remain open, look for end-results, and don't get caught up thinking there's only one answer, one solution. Remain open to serendipitous experiences. Even unfortunate occurrences can lead to fortuitous events that could not have been foreseen, or even consciously hoped for.

The secret is to remain open to new possibilities. Remain committed to your goals, but open up to better possibilities. When serendipity happens, *celebrate*. Set your sights, go into action, and keep your eyes open for your greater good.

Write down three serendipitous events that you've experienced:

1. _____

_____

2. _____

_____

3. _____

_____

Now, open yourself to synchronicity and start compiling a list of the serendipitous events that happen. Keep adding new instances as they occur.

_____

_____

_____

_____

_____

Chapter 18

Be Determined

(Strategy #12)

Success is a matter of not quitting and failure is a matter
of giving up too soon.   —Robert H. Schuller

After you've set your goal and gone into action, there will be
another force which will come, sometimes called the third
force, which somehow will endeavor to block the
achievement of your goal. This is only a test. If you exercise
persistence, determination, you'll pass the test and achieve your
goal.

When Henry Ford decided to produce his famous V-8 engine, he
chose to build an engine with the entire eight cylinders cast in one
block, and instructed his engineers to produce a design for the engine. The design was placed on paper, but the engineers all agreed
that it was simply *impossible* to cast an eight-cylinder engine block
in one piece.

Ford said, "Produce it anyway."

"But," they replied, "it's impossible!"

"Go ahead," Ford commanded, "and stay on the job until you
succeed, no matter how much time is required."

The engineers went ahead. There was nothing else for them to do
if they were to remain employed by Ford. Six months went by but
nothing happened. Another six months passed, and still nothing happened. Another six months passed, and still nothing happened. The
engineers tried every conceivable plan to carry out the order, but the
thing seemed out of the question. "It's *impossible!*" they cried.

At the end of the year, Ford checked with his engineers, and they
informed him they had found no way to carry out his order. "Go

right ahead," said Ford. "I want it, and I'll have it." They persevered and then, as if by a stroke of magic, the secret was discovered.

I've condensed the story, but the sum and substance of it is true. Research the story and see if you can find the secret of Ford's V8 engine. If you can do this, if you can lay your finger on the principles that made Henry Ford rich, you can equal his achievements in almost any calling for which you are suited.

Persevere

Those who win are those who persist. Why don't we persist? Why do we give up? We lack faith in our ability to triumph. We fail to believe in ourselves, what we are doing, and why we are doing it.

As the song goes, "You've got to know when to hold 'em and know when to fold 'em," but most of us fold 'em way too soon.

Of course, hanging on too long can be just as disastrous. What is the difference between persistence and stubbornness? Stubbornness tends to be negative, a resistance to change. Persistence generally is an effort to create a new and better way.

> *There's a power inside us that is the greatest force on*
> *Earth.* Oprah Winfrey

You can't blame the Better Business Bureau, your mother, or the President. Look inside yourself. Listen to the spirit. If you go into business without consulting your spirit, the business is doomed. Take Oprah Winfrey, for example. She was a lost little girl who dreamed big and worked hard. "I started out just a colored girl," she says. "It was a long way to being black."

By the time she was thirty-five, Winfrey was only the second woman, and the first African-American, to own her own television production studio. The first was comedienne Lucille Ball. Oprah's company, Harpo, Inc. (Oprah spelled backwards) had 1988 revenues of $80 million. She earned $37 million in 1986 and 1987 combined. Oprah's secrets are simple:

- If you're in it to make money, that's wrong. You have to believe in what you're doing.

- Treat people the way you want to be treated.

- Surround yourself with people who are better than you.
- If your people stab you in the back, rid yourself of them.
- Never give up your power to another person.

You must have a definite purpose backed by a burning desire for its fulfillment. You must have a definite plan expressed in continuous action, go into action. You must have a mind closed tightly against all negative influences including suggestions of friends, relatives and acquaintances. You must no longer be a party of the loser. Put them aside and join the winners. You must form a friendly alliance with one or more persons who will help you and encourage you to follow through with your plan or purpose.

> Let your mind speak these words with firm conviction: "If I persist and continue to try and continue to charge forward I will succeed. And I will persist until I succeed. The prizes of life are at the end of each journey, not at the beginning. And it is not given to me to know how many steps are necessary in order to reach my goals. Failure I may still encounter at the thousandth step, yet success hides behind the next bend in the road. never will I know how close it lies unless I turn the corner. Always will I take another step."
>
> —Jack Boland

Pick a goal that's worthy of your commitment, and give it consistent, persistent effort. Apply yourself with a relentless effort and your most optimistic predictions will be fulfilled You will be turbocharged.

> *Never give up, for that is just the place and time that the tide will turn.* —Harriet Beecher Stowe

I recently attended a money management seminar conducted by Greg, a local stockbroker. It's was a well-planned program, and at the end of the one-hour, box-luncheon program Greg asked for feedback and comments. One of the ladies said, "I've been flaky. It's been hard to get me here. You've had trouble—you've called me many times. I'm glad I finally attended. I'm glad you kept on calling. I learned a lot of important things." I, too, had received several invitations and had let other things take precedence over attending, and I, too, was glad I'd finally gotten around to it. However, the persistence Greg showed in sending out repeat invitation paid off in new clients.

Follow through and follow up. Don't let disappointments and turn-downs stop you from continuing to ask. Ask for what you want, not in a demanding, pushy way, but ask, ask, ask. Don't be surprised when more of what you want begins to come your way.

> *The world turns aside to let anyone pass who knows where they are going.* —David Starr Jordan

I'd been referred to John, a construction manager at the University of Washington, by Dave, one of my class members, a contractor who does work for the University of Washington. I called John on a Friday afternoon and, after a brief introduction, I said, "I'm in town and wonder if it would be possible to get together this afternoon?"

John said, "Yes," and off we went. We had a great meeting, and it should lead to lots of business for us and solve a lot of his problems. Roberta, an associate of mine, had a hard time believing that it's possible to see people in major organizations on the spur of the moment on a Friday afternoon.

Are you willing to ask for what you want? It all begins by asking. If you believe in it, if you believe in what you're doing, and if you believe it will help others solve their problems, what's stopping you from asking others to take the appropriate action? Ask for what you want. Begin by deciding what you want. Then ask, ask, ask for it. If you're disappointed, when the response isn't what you've asked for, keep on asking, asking, asking. Eventually, you'll gain an audience of enthusiastic participants. You'll get the cooperation of others. You'll reach your goals. You'll be turbo-charged.

What do you hesitate to ask for? _____

_____

_____

What do you need or want from others? _____

_____

When will you ask for it? _____

_____

> Sometimes I even look forward to the next failure. Your
> true test comes when you hit bottom.
> > —Bud Hadfield, co-founder and chairman
> > of Kwik Kopy Corp.

After two years of false attempts, I finally met with the president of an important construction company in Salem. We had a great visit, although he was a little cautious at first, which is to be expected. As the meeting unfolded, he was more and more willing to acknowledge the need for improvement in the skills of his important team members. At one point, he almost said, "Where have you been?" and I would have replied, "Knocking on your door."

The lesson I learned is the importance of persistent, intelligent effort. There are no results without persistent, intelligent effort. Effort alone is not the answer—intelligent effort is.

Be certain your efforts are intelligent. Develop additional skills whenever possible. Push your persistence ratio up. Knock on more doors; the results of your efforts will prove rewarding, and your self-confidence will be turbo-charged..

Don't Give Up

As I was digging, drilling, punching, pulling, trying to get a hole under my front sidewalk for the sprinkler system piping, my wife walked out, saw the pile of dirt, worried about her flower bed, and said, "Is all this necessary?"

I felt like quitting. I pushed harder instead, and pulled, hammered, twisted, until there was a clear hole for the pipe to go through. As I was digging and probing and punching and pulling, I thought of Robert Schuller's success creed, "When faced with a mountain, I will not quit. I will go over, under, around or through it, or simply stay and make a gold mine of it."

When the sprinkler system was finished, I turned it on, and heard the familiar *swish, swish.* Knowing that I hadn't quit made that *swish, swish* of the sprinkler sound like the sweet sound of success.

When you encounter mountains of unexpected deadlines, unscheduled breakdowns, incomplete orders, difficult prospects, uncooperative co-workers or suppliers, don't quit. Go over, under, around or through the problem, or find a way to make a gold mine of it. Whatever the sound, you'll hear the sweet tones of success.

> *It seems to me you have to stand a little rain if you want to see rainbows.*
> —Dolly Parton

Roger, the comptroller of a major paper mill, called to tell us he'd passed his C.M.A. (Certified Management Accountant; it's similar to a Certified Public Accountant, but far more practical for a person aiming to be a Chief Financial Officer inside a corporation rather than going into private practice as a C.P.A.). The C.M.A. designation is especially important to an accountant who wants to make meaningful contributions to the total quality management efforts of a firm. When I first met Roger two years ago, he was depressed, cynical, and negative. When he called to tell us about passing the C.M.A., he was full of himself, excited, optimistic. Why the difference in attitude? He'd set a goal and went after it with enthusiasm. He's more alive, more excited, more optimistic than ever.

If you would like to be more full of yourself, more alive, confident, and optimistic, set some goals for yourself, high stretching goals. How high would your goals be if you weren't afraid of failure? Robert Burns said, "Our goals should exceed our grasp, or what's a heaven for?" After you've set your goals, go after them as if you were a cat in pursuit of a mouse. You'll reach your goals, and, in the process, reach inside of yourself and find that greater you who's just hanging out waiting to be invited to the party.

> *I never allow myself to become discouraged under any circumstances. The three great essentials to achieve anything worthwhile are: first, hard work; second, stick-to-ittiveness; third, common sense.*
> —Thomas A. Edison

I set a world's record last weekend: I installed a gas dryer. I've never installed gas pipe before. Donna Lee had picked up the pipe a few days earlier, after our electric dryer burned out. We tried to put the new six-foot length of pipe into the new "T" and worked and worked and worked at it without success. We turned the pipe around and worked at it some more, still with no success.

Then, we tried the other six-foot length of pipe, and worked at it and worked at it with no success. We were fed up but turned the pipe around and it went in! We couldn't believe it. It was so easy. Character is the ability to carry out a resolution long after the mood has left you.

> *Nothing in the world can take the place of persistence. Talent will not; nothing is more common than unsuccessful men with talent. Genius will not; unrewarded genius is almost a proverb. Education will not; the world is full of educated derelicts. Persistence, and persistence alone, always will solve the problems of the human race.* —Calvin Coolidge

Have you achieved everything you've set out to achieve this week? Have you accomplished everything you'd hoped to accomplish? If not, give it one more persistent effort—one more try. Turn it around, try another angle. Try a new approach, and you will ultimately prevail. Have determination and you will succeed.

Bounce Back

Set backs are a part of life, and the higher your goals are, the greater number of attempts you make, the greater your chance of immediate failure and ultimate success. To cope with the immediate failure, you need a strategy for managing set backs. Here are ten tools to help you bounce back:

1. Be Your Own Best Friend. It's hard to bounce back if you're always down on yourself. A low self-image and the way you act because of it, sets you up for failure and disappointment. It creates a downward cycle that leads to sadness and depression and a feeling of not wanting to try again.

When you're honest with yourself, reflect on your past successes, and present yourself honestly to others, you start to feel good about yourself. You realize you are a good person, an important person. You'll broken that downward cycle, and you'll started to bounce back.

2. Be Realistic. There's nothing wrong with making big plans for the future, even if they sometimes get into the realm of pure fantasy, but it's important to keep your expectations realistic. For instance, reduced errors, improved productivity and teamwork are not automatic. That's going to take some effort on your part. But once you make up your mind about what you want and go after it, look out, world!

3. Pick Yourself Up. Most of the time you'll have to take the initiative to get yourself out of the dumps. Don't wait for a friend to call to cheer you up. You make the call. Sign up for an art class, take a tour of the city, try out for a play, invite friends to dinner. The important thing is not *what* you do, but that you *do something*. It's funny how when you look for the positive, you find it.

4. Give of Yourself. When you get involved with others and their problems, suddenly yours don't seem so overwhelming. Now that's bouncing back in the best of ways, because you're not the only one who benefits. And it can be as simple as being the listening ear for another's frustrations. Giving of yourself is the best gift of all, and it comes back in so many ways.

5. Give Yourself a Break. More often than not, people are more concerned with what's wrong with themselves than they are with what's wrong with you. They don't spend their time looking at you and trying to discover your weaknesses. The only real observer of your problems is you. And you know something? You're not half bad.

6. Get a Move On. Your life is precious. It's far too valuable to waste just sitting around. The more you do nothing, the more powerless you feel, and the more you'll feel that life is living you instead of the other way around.

7. Be Open. Talking about your problems is a good way to bounce back—especially when you can share them with a caring person, someone in your own family or a Master Mind group. These are people who love you. They care about what happens to you. They want to help.

Sure, sometimes it's hard to start these discussions because you're afraid they won't understand or they'll be disappointed in you. Yet, even though it might seem awkward at first, it's worth the effort. Your family, friends, or Master Mind Group can be a great source of comfort and reassurance when things get hard.

8. Accentuate the Positive. The way you look at a situation has a lot to do with how you respond to it. It's the old question of whether the glass is half full or half empty. A little creative thinking and a conscious effort to see things in a positive way can turn things around The ordinary becomes the extraordinary. A stumbling block becomes a stepping stone.

9. Learn from the Hard Times. Be glad for the challenges that come into your life. They're difficult to appreciate when you're trying to deal with them, but those are the times when you grow. Life is a series of good things and not so good things, and you need the bad to appreciate the good. Hard times build character. Negative events become positive lessons that better equip you to cope with future trials. And it's during the hard times that you really get to know yourself. You are forced to look closer at yourself to find the hidden reservoir of strength it takes to overcome adversity.

10. Realize You're Not Alone. The human spirit is remarkably resilient. We fall down—or get knocked down—yet somehow we manage to bounce back. But it can be hard. When disappointments crowd in on you, sometimes you feel alone and unable to go on, but when you look within yourself, way down deep inside, you come to the realization that you're really not alone at all.

"Character is the ability to carry out a resolution long after the mood has left you."

At the age of forty-two, George Sand, the famous 19th century French novelist, was a broken and depressed human being. (Like George Eliot, Sand adopted the male pseudonym to cover the fact that her novels were written by a woman.) Her personal life at this time had fallen apart and she was the victim of severe personal criticism from powerful and influential people in France.

One day, feeling low and melancholy, she wandered into the woods near her home where she had played as a child. Seated there on a boulder she thought over the past, pondered her future, and tried to analyze her personal situation. After a while, she reached a conclusion that was to enable her to go on and write another fifty plays and novels. That decision was this:

> *Henceforth I shall accept what I am and what I am not. With my limitations and my gifts, I shall go on using life as long as I am in this world and afterwards. Not to use life—that alone is death.*

Chapter 19

Be Flexible

(Strategy #13)

Patience is the companion of wisdom.

—St. Augustine

We arrived early to conduct a one-hour workshop for a major construction firm in Seattle. Sam, the General Manager invited us into his office. I had set the meeting up over the phone, and we'd never met. After the preliminary pleasantries, I asked Sam about his management team (its experience, strengths, areas for needed improvement, and so on). He started to tell me what he wanted me to cover during the meeting, but I'd already planned the meeting, I knew what needed to be covered and in what sequence.

How can we *all* reach our objectives, I asked myself, then said, "O.K., let's see how we can cover and accomplish the extra things you want covered." I didn't throw out my outline, I just told myself that I would find a way to fulfill Sam's requests. I started the program the way I always do and began to weave in the materials that would satisfy Sam. Then it happened! I found a way to make a point I'd been looking to make for months. It just came to me, popped in my head. It was fantastic! The group really got it—it was kinesthetic, guttural. They got it at a spinal level.

The lesson I learned is that when I trust myself, remain flexible and open, allow creativity to flow through and out, answers to problems float to the top.

Remain responsive to the requests of others, even when you aren't sure how you'll be able to do it. Be customer-driven. Trust your ability to respond. You'll find answers. You'll find abilities you didn't even know you possessed. Your win-win attitude will make you a winner.

> *Sometimes we stare so long at a door that is closing that we see too late the one that is open.*
> —Alexander Graham Bell

I conducted a morning management meeting at a restaurant in Eugene that is closed to the public until 11:00. The foyer was a little dark when we arrived, but I started the meeting on schedule at 7:00 a.m., even though the room was missing several people who'd registered for the event. About fifteen or twenty minutes into the meeting, a large group came into the room and explained why they were late. "The door was locked, and we couldn't get in. We tried the door, but it was locked."

When I had arrived, one door was indeed locked, but the other was open. Before leaving, I asked the hostess, who said, "Yes. One of the doors was locked." She only had the key for one door.

Either all these folks had tried one door, found it locked and assumed that the other door was locked as well, or one person had done so and announced to those who came after that the doors were locked and no one had tested his assumption.

Check every option before concluding that you're locked out, that you're limited, that you can't get in. Don't assume that if someone else tried and failed that you, too, will fail. Check every option before concluding, "There's no way!" Don't let others speak for you without verifying that "We can't do this!" Be skeptical of statements like, "This is impossible!" Instead of saying, "I am not able to participate!" try another door, try another option, try one more possibility.

Remember "baby steps"? Well, there's another step, a series of steps, actually, and it's more a dance than a step. It's one you'll find yourself doing involuntarily, for the most part. Most people have to dance their way to greatness, because the path is rarely a straight, line from point A to point B. More often, it's a progression of steps in a slow dance. You go forward three steps, then back two. Sometimes you go back two before you can advance three.

Unlock Doors

I swung into a gas station on my way back to the office and after refueling, I asked the attendant, "Where's the men's room?" He directed me around the building where I saw a unisex rest-room sign. I opened the door and was surprised to see a female attendant.

She blurted out something like, "I'm washing my hands."

I said, "Pardon me," closed the door and waited, and waited. It was cold, but I waited and waited and waited. I started pacing back and forth. It wasn't that urgent, though it could have been, but I was getting cold, and I was wondering and waiting. Finally, I went back inside to pay for the gas, and there was the female attendant.

It seems there was another door that led into the rest room from the inside, for employee use.

How much of our lives do we spend pacing around, waiting and wondering, and thinking that we're locked out of opportunities, barred, and excluded? The lesson I learned from this experience is to be certain of my assumptions before I conclude that I'm barred, locked out.

What opportunities would you like to take advantage of but hold back from thinking you're excluded? It might be something you've tried half-heartedly, or a situation where you experienced some resistance. Now you are waiting for an invitation! It's hard to see our self-imposed limitations; they seem so real! It's hard to realize that we are outside the door of opportunity. It takes some self-examination, honest exploration to really discover what doors are honestly locked and what doors only require one more small try to open—to swing wide open.

When you try one of those doors you assumed was locked, you'll discover that it swings open, and you can walk in. When you're stepping across the threshold, you'll experience a sense of relief which empowers you. You'll go on to the next, the next, and the next door. You'll be turbo-charged.

Find Solutions

We'd spent a lot of time and money promoting the Salem Leadership Lab, and we were still a long way from being able to start the class. Steve and I drove home from feeling disappointed, and when we got there Donna Lee started talking about the Leadership Lab and said, "Why don't you ..." And there lay the solution to our problem, a simple solution, right in front of me all the time. Steve and I had spent almost four hours discussing the problem on our drive to and from Eugene. We were so close to the problem that we couldn't see the solution, we couldn't see the forest for the trees.

The lesson I learned can be seen on the mud flaps back of many trucks where Yosemite Sam says, "Back Off." Sometimes, all we need to do is pull away from problems, reframe them. Include an innocent bystander in your problem-solving, a person who's interested but not bound up, not tied up, not locked into one way of thinking. So often we seem to think there's only one way, only one solution. As my friend, Dave Frackleton, says, "There are ten solutions to every problem, at least two of which are outstanding."

Pull back from your problems, your challenges. Do like the mud flap says and "Back off." Get away from your problems for a little while. Involve an interested, innocent bystander, a third party. You'll be amazed when you discover solutions that are far better than any you'd believed possible. Break the routine, try a new route, look at things through a child's eyes. Sometimes all that's needed to spark the solution to a nagging problem is the flexibility needed to look at things through someone else's eyes.

Do you remember this riddle: "I'm the son of a doctor who was killed in Vietnam, so when I was injured in a car accident and the policeman at the scene asked if there was a doctor in the crowd imagine my surprise when a doctor said he'd be happy to treat me because I was his son.

Question: Who was killed in Vietnam?
Answer: My mother.

Be open to new paradigms, new and different ways of seeing things. You'll be turbo-charged.

Chapter 20

Give Freely

(Strategy #14)

Successful people give. They don't give because they're successful; they're successful because they give. They don't give in the expectation that giving will make them rich. They give out of a spirit of generosity. They don't give for publicity or applause. They give in secret.

At the end of a two-week seminar in Crete, in response to the ritual, "Are there any questions?" he asked, "Dr. Papadorus, what is the meaning of life?" The usual laughter followed. People started to go. Papadorus held up his hand and stilled the room, looked at me for a long time, asking with his eyes if I was serious, and seeing from my eyes that I was, "I'll answer your question." Taking his wallet out of his hip pocket, he fished into the leather billfold and brought out a small, round mirror, about the size of a quarter. "When I was a small child during the war, one day, on the road, I found the broken pieces of a mirror. A German motorcycle had been wrecked in that place. I tried to find all the pieces and put them together, but that was not possible. So I kept only the largest piece—this one. And by scratching it on a stone, I made it round. I began to play with it as a toy, became fascinated by the fact that I could reflect light into dark places where the sun would never shine, in deep holes and crevices and dark closets. It became a game for me to get light into the most inaccessible places I could find. I kept the little mirror, and as I went about growing up, I would take it out and, in idle moments,

189

continue the challenge of the game. As I became a man, I grew to understand that this was not just a child's game but a metaphor for what I might do with my life. I came to understand that I am not the light or the source of light, but light, truth, understanding, knowledge is there, and it will only shine in many dark places if I reflect it. I am a fragment of a mirror whose whole design and shape I do not know. Nevertheless, with what I have I can reflect light into dark places of this world, into the black places, into the hearts of men, and change some things in some people. Perhaps others many see and do likewise. This is what I am about. This is the meaning of my life."

—Robert Fulghum, *It Was On Fire When I Lay Down On It*

We were getting reacquainted with an old friend recently when she began to tell us about the volunteering she does. She goes to the hospital once a week to hold cocaine babies. I could see a certain erectness, a certain pride, a certain confidence as she told us about the work she does. We are validated when we volunteer, and this gives us a sense of personal pride, confidence and enthusiasm.

Chances are you're already among the millions of Americans who each week volunteer their time. If so, congratulations. If not, find a way today to give a little back. You're never so tall as when you stoop to help another.

When you help someone it matters out of all proportion to how little it costs you. While Donna Lee was checking out at the office supply store, she handed a check to the clerk who tried to use it to cover her mouth as she sneezed uncontrollably. She said, sort of sniffling, "I wish I had a Kleenex." Donna Lee reached in her pocket and brought out a packet of tissue and handed it to her.

The clerk started to take a tissue out of the packet, and Donna Lee said, "No, you keep the whole packet." The young lady was so grateful, so thankful that someone had in this small way come to her aid, that Donna was delighted out of all proportion to what she'd done. Of all the things that happened in her life that day, the one thing that stood out most in her mind was the time when she freely, lovingly gave a little something extra to someone in need.

If you want to add to your joy and to the meaningfulness of your life, a simple way to do it is to find little things you can do for others. Performing these acts freely and without thought of reward, paradoxically, will reward you with much more than you give out.

Look for a way you can give a little more, a little extra. You may be amazed at what comes back to you. We live in an echo chamber, a house of mirrors, and you're reflection will be magnified and you'll be turbo-charged.

Victor Frankl, the eighty-seven-year-old author of the best-seller, *Man's Search For Meaning*, survived three grim years in Auschwitz and other Nazi prisons. Dr. Frankl gained freedom only to learn that almost his entire family had been wiped out.

Victor said that when he was a young boy of fifteen in Vienna, he concluded that if he could ever write anything that would make the world a better place, he didn't care who received the credit. Maybe it was this selfless attitude that helped him survive the tortures of Auschwitz and led to his being called "The greatest thinker since Freud and Adler."

St. Paul said, "Love covers a multitude of sins." Sin, literally interpreted, means "mistake." Mis-take. So don't worry about mistakes of the past; worry will rob you of any joy in the present. And, as you go about your day, don't be self-conscious about your actions or about making mistakes. Just put love before the course. Love will find a way. People will be amazed at your confidence, your spontaneity, your joy, and you will be lifted to new heights.

Shine a little light into the darkness, with a smile, with patient listening, with an understanding helping hand, and, as you do, you'll experience a lift, you'll be brighter, you'll be lighter.

Dedicate yourself to making your corner of the world a better place. There's no limit to what you can accomplish if you don't care who receives the credit.

Be Loving

Tom, one of the superintendents in our Salem Leadership Lab, made a loving presentation about the importance of open communication. At the end of his presentation, he called the class to action.

He said, "Find a way to express your feelings to those you love. Find a way to let them know you care." To dramatize his idea, he brought in three dozen yellow roses so that class members could take one home to show those they love how much they were appreciated. When I took mine home, Donna Lee was thrilled to see it.

Have you found a way to express your appreciation, your affection? Who do you care about, and what will you do to dramatize how you feel toward them? Why not buy some yellow roses. Who do you think got the most benefit out of those yellow roses? Well, I think Tom did. By taking a dramatic stand for expressing feelings of love, appreciation and affection for others, Tom was himself empowered to express more of his feelings of love, admiration and respect for those he loves.

> *It is something to be able to paint a particular picture, or to create a statue and so to make a few object beautiful; but it is far more glorious to carve and paint the very atmosphere and medium through which we look...to affect the quality of the day—that is the highest of arts.* —Henry David Thoreau

Our youngest son returned home, and I cleaned out a bedroom closet to make it easier for him to get moved in. I'd wanted to clean that closet out for months. We took four bags of outdated clothes to the Salvation Army. It felt great to clean things out and to give things away.

Do you want a little lift, do you want to be a little lighter and brighter? Clean out a closet and give something away. You'll feel cleaner and lighter, you'll be exercising the law of circulation, and you'll open up a space for more good to come into your life.

Live Fully

I attended a memorial service for my close friend of twenty years, Jack Boland, and it turned out to be one of the most unusual experiences of my life. During part of the service we watched a video of Jack conducting his own memorial service, taped about ten days before his transition. He was, as he said, "As much alive, today, as I've ever been." And then he read John Quincy Adams' letter to Thomas Jefferson three days before he died.

> *John Quincy Adams is well, but the house in which he lives at the present time is becoming dilapidated. It is tottering on his foundations. Time and the seasons have nearly destroyed it. Its roof is pretty well worn out. Its walls are mud-shattered and tremble with every wind. I think John Adams will have to move out of it very soon, but he himself is quite well.*

Can you say, "I have never been better in my life?" As you develop your ability to live life fully, in spite of the fact that it's the morning, or Monday, or you have a cold, or you have bills pressing upon you, or you have loved ones for whom you are concerned, as you learn to live every precious, priceless minute to its fullest with love and intention, you will be fully alive every minute that you live, and you will communicate that aliveness even after you have passed away.

The famous psychiatrist, Dr. Karl Menninger, was answering questions from the audience following a lecture on mental health. One man asked, "What would you advise a person to do, if that person felt a nervous breakdown coming on?"

The audience expected him to reply: "Consult a psychiatrist." To their astonishment, he replied: "Lock up your house, go across the railway tracks, find someone in need and do something to help that person."

The Man In The Glass

When you get what you want in your struggle for self
And the world makes you king for a day.
Just go to a mirror and look and at yourself
And see what that man has to say.

For it isn't your father or mother or wife
Whose judgment upon you must pass;
The fellow whose verdict counts most in your life
Is the one staring back from the glass.

Some people may think you a straight-shootin' chum
And call you a wonderful guy.
But the man in the glass says you're only a bum
If you can't look him straight in the eye.

He's the fellow to please, never mind all the rest.
For he's with you clear up to the end.
And you've passed your most dangerous, difficult test.
If the man in the glass is your friend.

You may fool the whole world down the pathway of life.
And get pats on your back as you pass;
But your final reward will be heartaches and strife
If you've cheated the man in the glass.

My wish for you is that you come to know yourself even more in the light of your strengths in the year that lies ahead. As you see yourself even more clearly in terms of your true strengths you will find the acceptance of others, though always nice to receive, not a requirement for your self-esteem, motivation, or direction. This will make you even more self-motivated and you will choose your own goals and propel yourself towards them.

To become even more aware of your strengths and to gain greater insights into your goals, keep a record of your successes. Record them each day, no matter how trivial they may seem. Fill each section with your most meaningful accomplishment for that day. Note your accomplishments in the table below using the following keys:

"P" for a Physical Accomplishment $ for a Financial Accomplishment
"F" for a Familial Accomplishment   "S" for a Social Accomplishment
"C" for a Career Accomplishment   "*" for a Spiritual Accomplishment

My Record of Successes

Date	Key	Success	Personal Quality Demonstrated

Success

To laugh often and much;

To win the respect of intelligent people and affection of children;

To earn the appreciation of honest critics and endure the betrayal of false friends;

To appreciate beauty, to find the best in others;

To leave the world a bit better, whether by a healthy child, a garden patch or a redeemed social condition;

To know even one life has breathed easier because you have lived

This is to have succeeded.

About the Author

Larry W. Dennis is the energetic founder of Turbo Management Systems.™ The author of the successful books, *Repeat Business* and *Empowering Leadership,* shares the philosophy behind his ability to improve profits for hundreds of businesses whose key managers have learned the important principles of Empowering Leadership and Superior Customer Service. Through his company, Dennis has been responsible for improving the profits of hundreds of businesses whose key managers have learned the important principles of repeat business practices. Dennis is also the inventor of the patented video training system, Psycho-Actualized Learning, and is a dedicated father who has been profiled in "Secrets of Raising Teenagers Successfully." He is listed in *Who's Who of the World,* and he serves on the Business Advisory Council of Warner Pacific College.

THE SERVICES OF
TURBO MANAGEMENT SYSTEMS™

Partnering

"Putting the handshake back into construction."

Partnering is a proactive process used to overcome the adversarial relationships that have built up among contractors and owners over the years. Lower costs, improve morale, enhance quality.

Leadership Development Lab

"Bringing out the best so results exceed high expectations."

A 10-session program to build lasting leadership qualities. You integrate into your style improved approaches to bringing out the best in all people situations. Includes goal setting, team-building, problem-solving, and more.

Cultural Quality Awareness

To achieve "World Class" performance there must be a starting point—a "Milestone Day!" Designed to overcome the natural resistance to change and create momentum. Your team will leave the event with a clear understanding of why the culture must change, and action steps to make it happen.

Management Team Advance

Re-energize your management team, and every member on it! The objective of the MTA is to help each member of your management team BUILD on their strengths and ACT upon vital strategies and action programs developed during the advance to create a breakthrough in their performance and contribution to the team.

Comprehensive Organizational Analysis

The COA is a simple procedure that scales the strengths and weaknesses of your company and suggests priority actions that can immediately improve performance, reduce costs and improve quality over a period of time.

For more information about Turbo Management Systems,™ Management Team Advance, Cultural Quality Awareness, Leadership Development Lab, or Team Management Training contact:

Turbo Management Systems™

5440 S. W. Westgate Drive, Suite 340

Portland, Oregon 97221

Telephone: 503-292-1919

Fax: 503-292-2118

Repeat Business

by Larry W. Dennis

In straightforward, plain language and colorful anecdotes, Larry explains how to...

- Follow Through

- Remember Customers' Names

- Use the Telephone Effectively

- Project a Helpful Attitude

- Add Personal Excellence To Every Transaction

- Make Every Customer Feel Important

- Recover With Complaining Customers

Read what businesspeople say about *Repeat Business* and you'll understand why it's a book for everyone who depends on customers for a livelihood. And that includes all of us.

Not since the *One Minute Manager* has a simple little book made such perfect sense. As one reviewer wrote: "It's so enjoyable and easy to read...a cross between Garrison Keillor and Paul Harvey...But most of all it got me excited about what we can do to create repeat business."

Another reader said, "It's a wow of a book...As you read, master and apply the principles the author has introduced, you will wow yourself with the amount of business you will create and repeatedly serve."

Repeat Business is a book companies want extra copies of for every employee. It's the book to have on hand to remind you about the things that keep customers happy and keep them coming back.

This book is designed to be used as a guide for weekly customer service meetings.

Every employee will have their copy, and the manager will use the book as a guide for a stimulating meeting that results in *Superior Customer Service.*®

> **"Repeat Business** *is an excellent road map for the new manager whose success in business relies on customer service (That's all of us!)..."*
>
> —Don Olsen, publisher, This Week Magazine

> *"It's so enjoyable and easy to read...a cross between Garrison Keillor and Paul Harvey...But most of all it got me excited about what we can do to create repeat business. I want to make sure every employee in my office has a copy."*
>
> —Nada S. Perrie, general manager, GTE Mobilnet

Use the order form in the back of the book
or order by fax (503) 292-2118 or phone (503) 292-1919

Second big printing   ISBN 0-9631766-0-9 $12.95

EMPOWERING LEADERSHIP

by Larry W. Dennis

Enlightened 21st Century leaders know that their primary responsibility is building people and making them successful. In EMPOWERING LEADERSHIP, Larry W. Dennis helps you understand the fundamental leadership principles needed to tap your team's potential.

EMPOWERING LEADERSHIP PROVIDES:

- Distinguishing Characteristics of a Leader

- An Overview of the Total Quality Management Movement

- Ways of Creating Synergistic Teamwork

- Six Steps to Practical Problem Solving

- Ways to Challenge Change

- 3-Steps to Coaching Champions

- The 15 Fundamental Leadership Principles

- Tools to Solve Problems As a Team

- Ways to Tap the Creativity of Your Team

Written with hundreds of real life examples, in an entertaining, easy-to-read style, you will find meaningful information and inspiration on every page.

"The thing that I appreciate most about EMPOWERING LEADERSHIP is that the principles are so clearly defined and so easy to follow."

—Ed Adkins, salesman, Ivy Hi-Lift

"*The insight you present in EMPOWERING LEADERSHIP has given our management team the clear and precise ability to develop their leadership skills.*"
—Walter H. Smith, president, Active Construction, Inc.

"*EMPOWERING LEADERSHIP taught me that I can make a positive change in the business and personal lives of my team.*"
—Todd Hess, president, The Todd Hess Building Company

"*The fifteen principles of leadership in your book are like spark plugs of power that give readers the boost they need to take action.*"
—Kathy Dietrich, general manager, Architects Associate

"*Page after page the wisdom of your book provides valuable tools I apply daily to raise our team to higher levels of accomplishment.*"
—Ron Warman, general manager, Ron's Automotive

Use the order form in the back of the book
or order by fax (503) 292-2118 or phone (503) 292-1919

ISBN 0-9631766-1-7   294 pages $14.95

REMEMBERING NAMES AND MORE

VIDEO

A THREE-COURSE MEMORY SYSTEM

1. NAMES

2. HOOKING

3. BYTES

With what you learn on this video, you will impress other, achieve recognition, prove your reliability, and gain the favorable attention of others.

This video features the only U.S. Patented system for video production. It has been tested with over 5,000 people and has proven to achieve astounding results. You can surpass your expectations. You can remember names and more. Don't just watch this video. Practice its principles daily. YOU WILL AMAZE YOURSELF.

Anyone Can Juggle

A 27-Minute Video by Barry A. Dennis

Juggle in 3 easy steps
Fun for all ages
Includes 3 Juggle Bags
Music Video included for inspiration

"Clever...& infectious in its charm."
—Video Librarian, April 1991

Available for $19.95. Use the order form on the next page
or order by fax (503) 292-2118 or phone (503) 292-1919

Order form

Please send me

    _____ copies of *Empowering Leadership* @ $14.95 each
    _____ copies of *Repeat Business* @ $11.95
    _____ copies of *How To Turbo-Charge You* @ $14.95
    _____ copies of *Communicating For Results* @ $9.95
    _____ copies of *Making Moments Matter* @ $9.95
    _____ videos of *Remembering Names and More* @ $69.95
    _____ videos of *Anyone Can Juggle* @ $19.95
    _____ *Turbo Presentations* demo videos @ $19.95
    _____ Empowering Leadership Baseball Caps @ $9.95

☐ Please send me at no charge complete information about the training services of Turbo Management Systems.™

Please add $2.00 shipping and handling for first item and $1.00 for each additional item, for a total amount of $_____.

☐ Check enclosed   ☐ Bill my MasterCard/VISA

Account # _____

Expires_____ Signature _____

Ship to (Please allow 4-6 weeks for delivery):
Name: _____
Address:_____
_____
City/State/Zip: _____
Phone: _____

Mail or Fax your order to:
Turbo Management Systems™
5440 S. W. Westgate Drive, Suite 340
Portland, Oregon 97221
Phone: 503-292-1919   Fax: 503-292-2118